Mary of Magdala

Mary of Magdala

What *The Da Vinci Code* Misses

Mary R. Thompson

Paulist Press
New York/Mahwah, N.J.

Cover design by Trudi Gershenov

Library of Congress Cataloging-in-Publication Data

Thompson, Mary R., 1928-
    Mary of Magdala : what The Da Vinci code misses / Mary R. Thompson. — Rev. ed.
        p. cm.
    Includes bibliographical references and index.
    ISBN 0-8091-4380-1 (alk. paper)
    1. Mary Magdalene, Saint. I. Title.
    BS2485.T47 2006
    226'.092—dc22

                                                                    2005020579

Published by Paulist Press
997 Macarthur Boulevard
Mahwah, NJ 07430

www.paulistpress.com

Printed and bound in the
United States of America

Contents

CONTENTS

Acknowledgments

The inspiration for this study came from a series of lectures given by Dr. C. F. D. Moule at McMaster University in Hamilton, Ontario. The marked prominence of Mary of Magdala in the four crucifixion and empty-tomb narratives seemed to indicate that she held importance in the early church. Even a cursory examination of the apocryphal literature added conviction about her role. Dr. Moule encouraged further investigation. This book is the result.

I am deeply indebted to the Congregation of the Sisters of St. Mary of Namur for allowing me the time and providing the encouragement for this enterprise. I am grateful to the editorial staff at Paulist Press for valuable assistance and encouragement.

INTRODUCTION

Why Mary of Magdala?

Who was Mary of Magdala? What role did she play in the life of the early Christian communities? Was she an apostle, a disciple, a leader of the apostolic community? Was she the same Mary of Magdala who came to be known as a sinner, a prostitute? Was she beloved of Jesus and highly respected in the earliest days of the infant church or was she a great sinner who repented greatly? What was her personal relationship to Jesus? Could they have been married?[1] The fourth gospel tells us that Jesus revealed to Mary alone the fact that he had risen. He entrusted to her the task of relaying this great mystery to his other disciples who were huddled in an upper room for fear of being identified as his followers. On the other hand, for centuries the name of Mary Magdalene has referred to a prostitute whose great sin had been forgiven because of her great sorrow. The magnitude of this picture of the prostitute has even penetrated our language. The word "Magdalene" has long been ascribed to an unmarried woman who became pregnant. The word "maudlin" is a British contraction of that word.

Historical development through the ages of the apocryphal writings, the Fathers of the Church, the Middle Ages, the Reformation and the modern era is strewn with conflicting, complementary and complimentary descriptions of this enigmatic woman. The influence of allegorizing, mythologizing and outright romanticizing brings echoes of the triple goddess Mari-Anna-Ishtar, of the bride of the Song of Songs, of the Sophia-Wisdom figure, of all the goddesses of Love, even of the mother of Jesus. "The Magdalene embodies the paradoxical ideas of the feminine as the source and destroyer of life, as the dangerous but fascinating seducer of men, as the pure spirit, Sophia-Wisdom," as Marjory Malvern has written.[2]

It is no wonder that the Magdalene has held the attention of women through the ages. She exemplifies contemplation, penitence, ardent devotion, pure love. It is no wonder that the Magdalene has also held the attention of men through the ages. She exemplifies a radical dualism of carnal and spiritual love: she can be castigated as a prostitute and admired as a penitent. She can be observed in a more human way than traditionally has been allowed to Mary, the mother of Jesus, who has been progressively removed from human existence to some type of transcendent reality.

In spite of the opposing images, it is possible to detect a clear line of development in the picture of Mary of Magdala through the ages. With minor variations, the synoptic gospels tell the same story—Mary and her companions were witnesses to the crucifixion and burial of Jesus. They went out early on the morning of the third day and discovered that the tomb was empty. The fourth gospel adds the element of apostleship—Mary encountered the risen Lord and he sent her to proclaim his resurrection to the other disciples. In the first century of the church's mission, the attitude toward Mary of Magdala was very clear, very laudatory and totally consistent.

In the postapostolic age, apocryphal writings—by and large gnostic but not entirely so—presented an even more laudatory picture of Mary of Magdala. She had been the primary witness to the resurrection who, by that fact, was accorded respect and authority. She regularly challenged Peter and often had the better of the argument. She is pictured as having been much loved by

Jesus even though Peter and some others voiced objection to this preference. In the noncanonical writings from the first to the end of the third century, Mary of Magdala remained a dominant and revered person.

The Council of Nicaea in 325 CE was part of a radical turning point in the history of the church. When the Emperor Constantine decreed that Christianity was to be the religion of the Empire, realities and perceptions of realities began to change—especially in regard to the role that women had been playing in the church. Another related and important reality that changed was the position of the clergy. In a society becoming ever more hierarchical in philosophy as well as in fact, the clergy grew more and more separated from the laity and, as a result, a clerical state began to emerge. In order for the male clergy to achieve the power and prestige necessary to survive in the hierarchicalized Roman Empire, division between clergy and laity seemed to become necessary and the power of women had to be minimized. Stories of great women were modified or even eliminated.

In the popular novel *The Da Vinci Code,* Dan Brown, referring to the time when women were "put in their place," wrote rather facilely,

> The Priory believes that Constantine and his male successors successfully converted the world from "matriarchal paganism" to "patriarchal Christianity" by waging "a campaign of propaganda that demonized the sacred feminine, obliterating the goddess from modern religion forever."[3]

Brown's book is fiction and as such, can manufacture facts at will. However, this book claims to present realities such as *The Priory of Sion* as historically accurate. This creates the kinds of difficulties found in the above quotation. It is indisputably true that

Christianity underwent radical change before, during and after Constantine's reign. To speak of a change from "matriarchal paganism" to "patriarchal Christianity" is, at best, an exaggeration. The "campaign of demonizing propaganda and goddess obliteration" is totally fictional. This method of admixing fact, exaggeration and fiction does little service to those attempting to portray Mary of Magdala as a living human being in Jesus' time or as the symbolic figure she became in the early church.

The church in the eastern part of the Empire was able to maintain the canonical gospel portrait of Mary of Magdala largely by maintaining that the three women of the gospels, Mary of Bethany, the sinful woman of Luke 7 and Mary of Magdala were three different persons. To this day the eastern churches revere Mary as a holy woman who carried the message of resurrection to the other disciples. Marina Warner observed correctly, "The Greek Church followed the exegesis of Origen and always distinguished three separate women: Mary of Bethany, Lazarus' sister; Mary Magdalene, the witness of the resurrection; and the sinner."[4] It is only in the conflation of these three women that Mary of Magdala could be considered a prostitute.

In the West the situation was different. Jerome, who can hardly be considered objective about the roles of women, does not clearly conflate Mary of Bethany with Mary of Magdala: "Read the Gospel and see how Mary, seated at the Lord's feet, is preferred to busy Martha....Be thou also a Mary. Prefer instruction to food."[5] In the midst of much allegorizing there seems to be great reluctance on the part of Ambrose, Jerome and even Augustine to identify the two anointers, Mary of Bethany and the sinful woman of Luke's gospel, let alone include Mary of Magdala in the composite. Eventually Augustine came to the conclusion that there was, indeed, one woman who performed the anointing of Jesus' feet. He believed that the one story is recounted in two different gospels (Luke

7:36–50 and John 12:1–11). Whether or not this gave impetus to moving further and identifying the sinful woman with Mary of Magdala is unclear in Augustine's time. However, it is clear that it had been accomplished by the time of Gregory the Great (c. 540–604 CE). Somehow, in the time between the third century and the time of Gregory, the composite Mary Magdalene had become the accepted portrait in the western churches. Gregory wrote, "This woman, whom Luke called the sinful woman, whom John calls Mary, we believe to be that Mary of whom Mark affirms that she was delivered of seven demons."[6] The composite Magdalene, the combined figure—the sinful woman, Mary of Bethany and witness to the resurrection—is firmly in place in the western church by the end of the sixth century.

Involved in the evolution of the composite Magdalene, and in the legends and devotions which grew up around her, is the random confusion of Marys described by St. Cyril of Jerusalem in the fourth century: "I am Mary Magdalene because the name of the village where I was born was Magdalia. My name is Mary of Cleopa. I am Mary of James son of Joseph the carpenter."[7] In discussing this writing of Cyril, Montague James refers to it as a reckless identification of Marys. The lack of precision is noteworthy because it explains something of the ease by which the primary witness of resurrection could be made into a harlot. It might also contribute to the perplexing question of the ambiguities that occur between Mary, the mother of Jesus, and Mary of Magdala in the later apocrypha.

Allegorized scripture commentary and romanticized religious practices contributed to the medieval, ill-informed, conflated picture of Mary of Magdala, the prostitute. By the seventh century, Mary Magdalene was honored at Ephesus on July 22, the date on which she is reported to have died there. The legend from Ephesus describes John the Evangelist having come to Ephesus with Mary.

Sometime early in her life she was alleged to have been in love with John. She became so distraught when he followed Jesus that she gave herself up to a life of prostitution. This ended when she, too, became committed to following Jesus. According to this charming but totally imaginary legend, after the crucifixion and death of Jesus, John and Mary married and returned to preach and teach in Ephesus. The story is typical of legendary materials that circulated after the conflation of the three Marys had become accepted usage. It is founded upon a belief, legendary though it is, in the existence of a relationship between Mary of Magdala and John, the disciple of Jesus.

The legends, fantasies and miracles that surrounded devotion to Mary of Magdala in southern France in the eleventh and twelfth centuries are startling and indicative of thought patterns and customs in the Middle Ages. In the midst of a great deal of high-blown romanticism, there is still no hint that Mary of Magdala was Jesus' wife. According to one legend recorded by Jacobus de Voragine in the most famous source of information from this period, *The Golden Legend*, the arm of Mary of Magdala "tightly wrapped in cloth bandages was displayed to St. Hugh of Lincoln at the Abbey of Fecamp."[8] A tale was told of a knight having been raised from the dead through Mary of Magdala's intercession. Among other strange achievements, Mary is said to have been fed by angels, to have cured blindness and to have set prisoners free. She is reported to have died on Easter Sunday after having received communion and "such was the perfume of her sanctity that for seven days the oratory was filled with it."[9]

In the tenth and eleventh centuries, a multiplication of shrines and relics occurred throughout Europe. In England, the cathedral of Exeter had a shrine to Mary Magdalene by the eleventh century and claimed to have Mary's finger as a relic. "The problem [of miracles being worked through false relics venerated in ignorance] caused embarrassment only when two churches claimed to possess the same relics," says Jonathan Sumption.[10] The rapid spread of devotion to Mary of Magdala and of shrines and relics eventually replaced devotion to the apostles and even to the mother of Jesus.

The forces that had blended Mary Magdalene into the penitent harlot came to a climax in southern France. The fervor over the penitent prostitute lasted until the Reformation and in some places long beyond that. Some elements of this fervor have lasted into the twentieth century. After the conflation of the three gospel women into the one person of the Magdalene, all of the seeds for allegorizing, legendizing and moralizing were in place. Voragine wrote:

> Mary is interpreted "amarum mare," bitter sea, or light-giver, or enlightened. By these three things are understood the three best parts which she chose, namely the part of penance, the part of inward contemplation, and the part of heavenly glory.[11]

The composite is complete and unquestioned. Much had changed since the works of Origen, Ambrose, Jerome and Augustine who insisted upon the separation of the three women.

When Voragine had inherited the composite figure, he launched into a highly dramatic and totally fictionalized life of Mary Magdalene, sister of Lazarus and Martha, from her time in Galilee to her sojourn in Judea and then to her abandonment "to the pleasures of the senses."[12] Her parents, Voragine wrote, were noble and even of royal lineage. They had large possessions, the geography of which is astounding. After describing her role in the crucifixion, burial and resurrection very briefly, Voragine proceeds to describe the time fourteen years after her death:

> In the fourteenth year after the Passion and Ascension of Our Lord, the disciples went out into the divers regions of the earth to sow the word of God; and Saint Peter entrusted Mary Magdalene

to Saint Maximinus, one of the seventy-two disciples of the Lord. Then Saint Maximinus, Mary Magdalene, Lazarus, Martha, Martilla, and Saint Cedonius, the man born blind who had been cured by Jesus, together with still other Christians were thrown by the infidels into a ship without a rudder and launched into the deep, in the hope that in this way they would all be drowned at once. But the ship was guided by the power of God and made port in good estate at Marseilles.[13]

The narrative explains handily how the body of Mary Magdalene came to be interred in France. Three locales of southern France are mentioned as shrines containing bones of Mary Magdalene—Sainte-Baume, Vézelay and Saint Maximin in Provence. "In the mid-eleventh century, under extremely—as some would say, suspiciously—obscure circumstances, the monks of Vézelay discovered that they had the body of the Madeleine."[14] The stage was set for intense rivalry when another set of relics of Mary Magdalene was found at Saint Maximin in Provence.

Exaggerated legends and devotions flourished throughout the Middle Ages. Churches were dedicated to Mary Magdalene: Victor Saxer lists 33 shrines to Marie Madeleine in the High Middle Ages, 80 such shrines in the eleventh century, 91 in the early twelfth century and 130 in the late twelfth century (1150–1199).[15] Among those shrines are several important to this study, the Basilique de la Madeleine at Vézelay, the cathedral at Exeter in England and l'Église Sainte Madeleine in Paris. In tenth-century England, the rebirth of literary drama began with the enactment of the "Quem Quaeritis" trope, the story of Mary Magdalene meeting Jesus at the scene of the empty tomb. She is depicted in the mystery plays such as "Mary Magdalene" of the *Digby Mysteries.*

Biographies of Mary Magdalene became popular in the Middle Ages and early Renaissance—the best known is probably the previously mentioned account found in *The Golden Legend* of Jacobus de Voragine. Still extant are copies of Jean Misrahi's *Vita Sanctae Mariae Magdalenae* and Robert Reinsch's edition of *La Vie de Madeleine of Guillaume le Clercq*. Early in the Middle Ages (c. 800 CE) *The Life of Saint Mary Magdalene and Her Sister Saint Martha* appeared, attributed to Rabanus Maurus, Archbishop of Mainz.

From late medieval and Renaissance artists came almost innumerable works for which Mary Magdalene was the inspiration; those of Bellini, Perugino, Botticelli, Donatello, Correggio, Titian and others. It is, indeed, an enigma that such a simple gospel portrait of three separate women could become fused into one woman who becomes a worldwide source of piety, devotion and art.

The excesses of the Middle Ages helped to bring on the castigations of the Reformers. However, in spite of the Reformers' efforts to purify, simplify and correct the extravagances that characterized the devotions and preaching of the time, the appeal of Mary Magdalene both in popular devotion and in artistic expression continues. As recently as the rock opera of the 1960s, *Jesus Christ Superstar,* and the filming in the late 1980s of Nikos Kazantzakis's *The Last Temptation of Christ,* the portrait of Mary Magdalene, the penitent harlot, has been retained. *The Da Vinci Code* is ambiguous about the relationship between Jesus and Mary of Magdala, but has become very popular. The advent of scientific exegesis has begun to unravel the picture of the composite Mary Magdalene and to restore some of the pre-Gregorian understanding of a woman who was a friend of Jesus, loyal disciple, leader among early Christians and primary witness to the resurrection. The following chapters intend to contribute to that restoration by examining the real evidence about Mary of Magdala in the canonical gospels and in the apocrypha, in an attempt to restore the unmythologized, unlegendized, unromanticized depiction of Mary of Magdala.

So, to answer the questions raised at the beginning of this introduction, who was Mary of Magdala? First and foremost, she was a devoted follower of Jesus. For almost 300 years she was acknowledged as an important leader. Even when she had become a symbol of a specific nonhierarchical trend in the early communities, she maintained a prominence that sometimes placed her in opposition to the trend symbolized by the presentations of Peter in the apocryphal writings. Her role in the life of the early Christian community seems to have been that of leader who represented everyone in the communities, not just the women. There is no hint of any kind of division found in the documents. Clearly, she was *not a prostitute*. She had been made to seem that by the conflation of three different women into one figure. Her personal relationship to Jesus can be discerned only to a limited extent. She was clearly devoted to him, so much so that she went out on the morning of the third day to find the crucified body of Jesus. She had obviously been a follower who, with other women, supported Jesus and his followers out of their own resources. Any further description of her and her relationships is unsupportable conjecture.

CHAPTER 1

Related Questions

Mary of Magdala was so prominent a member of the early Christian community that it was impossible for writers to eliminate her name from the resurrection narratives. To allow her name to be eliminated from the narrative would have been comparable to writing the story of the American Revolution without mentioning George Washington. Mary's influence had become so widespread that it remained a significant part of the narratives for at least three centuries, during which time she became a symbol of a nonhierarchical understanding of church. Her importance in the early community explains the consistency of the gospel writers who included her in all of their crucifixion and resurrection accounts.

Literary Background

To achieve a balanced portrait, it is important to delve into the contemporary literary and religious factors that influenced the formation of the portrait of Mary of Magdala. In the gospel portrayals of Mary are found echoes of the mythology of the goddess, of the concept of the "sacred feminine" and of the Sophia-Wisdom figure of the Old Testament. The concept that includes the others is that of the "sacred feminine," commonly understood in three ways:

1. As an androgynous figure in which male and female are totally present
2. As the feminine aspect of deity

3. As a fully human being with echoes of divine characteristics

In the canonical gospels, Mary of Magdala clearly reflects the third
of these aspects. She is totally devoted to Jesus, she is the leader of
the women, she is able to see and comprehend the meaning of the
resurrection of Jesus. The picture changes in the noncanonical literature. There she acquires all three dimensions of the "sacred feminine." She can demonstrate male characteristics while remaining
female, as in the dialog in the Coptic *Gospel of Thomas* where Jesus
promises to make Mary male.[1] She knows the All, surely a divine
prerogative, and she is fully human. She weeps outside the tomb,
she brings the others to the tomb, she provides for the needs of others from her own wealth. The portrayal in the noncanonical literature clearly indicates an echo of the "sacred feminine." Mythology
was in the air during the first and second centuries. Echoes of the
Egyptian goddess Isis, weeping at the death of her spouse and son
and then resuscitating him, can be heard in the canonical and noncanonical portrayals. The Syrian goddess Ishtar, the shepherd
Tammuz, and the Canaanite goddess Anat who annually married
the god Baal, also echo in the picture of Mary following the beloved
shepherd and weeping outside the empty tomb.

There is also a trajectory from the Sophia-Wisdom figure of the
Hebrew scriptures to the gospel portrait of Mary of Magdala. In the
Hebrew scriptures, the figure of Wisdom is a woman (Proverbs 1–8,
Sirach 1:1–8 and so forth). The Hebrew scripture portrayal of
Sophia-Wisdom echoes all three of the dimensions of the "sacred
feminine," but the gospel picture of Mary avoids direct reference to
divinity and concentrates on the fully human being who demonstrates total devotion and persistence. The writers of the apocryphal gospels had no such inhibitions. Their portrait often

confused the very human picture of Mary in the canonical gospels with one or more aspects of the "sacred feminine."

An interesting recent development in the portrayal of Mary of Magdala has been the effort to insert Mary of Magdala into the medieval English tradition of the Holy Grail. Following Baignet's *Holy Blood, Holy Grail* and Dan Brown's *The Da Vinci Code*, this contention has become part of popular understanding. Introducing the Holy Grail into the story of Mary of Magdala requires a tremendous stretch of the imagination, since the Holy Grail, in its original meaning as the cup from which Jesus drank at the Last Supper and in which Nicodemus is said to have collected some of the blood dripping from the cross of Jesus, appears for the first time in the Arthurian legends of England around the late twelfth century. It is relevant that those legends were themselves in a process of development all during the twelfth and thirteenth centuries. It seems somewhat fanciful to suggest that, after twelve centuries, the Holy Grail could rather peremptorily become part of the traditions about Mary of Magdala. There also exists a significant geographical divide between the British Isles and Palestine, not to mention the morphing from a cup to a human being. The original quest for the Holy Grail (that almost certainly had its beginnings in Celtic mythology as a journey narrative in search of the cup) has had a vibrant career of its own. It is impossible to associate this legend with the historical Mary of Magdala or even with the symbolic figure of the noncanonical gospels.

Jesus and Mary of Magdala

At the beginning of this twenty-first century a very significant interest in things religious has become apparent. Celebrities publicize New Age beliefs. Thousands flock to view *The Passion of the Christ* and many more thousands have read *The Da Vinci Code*. Even though a multiplicity of motives lies behind these phenomena, they indicate some growing interest in things religious in our society. One questionable theory that has arisen from this popularization of religious issues is the question of the relationship between Jesus and Mary of Magdala.[2] In *The Da Vinci Code* Brown has created a tidal wave of concern over this matter. One of the few arguments for a very close relationship is founded on the gnostic Gospel of Philip, "There were three who always walked with the Lord: Mary, his mother, her sister, and Mary Magdalene, the one who was called companion."[3] Here, the Greek word *koinonos,* which is translated as "companion," can also mean "partner" or "consort." In the same gospel is found the passage, "But Christ loved her more than all the disciples and used to kiss her often on the lips."[4] Since there is not a hint of such a relationship in the canonical gospels, the above quotations need to be understood as part of a highly romanticized and fictional picture based on the composite figure of three women conflated into the understanding of Mary Magdalene as the repentant sinner. Clearly, they reflect the excessive sentimentality of the medieval age. There is no credible evidence that such a marriage ever took place albeit there is none that it did not. It makes no difference which of the statements comes closer to the reality, but in none of the literature is it said, and the tradition of centuries is against the probability of such a marriage ever having taken place.

The "Sinful Woman"

The most important working principle in discerning the role of Mary of Magdala in the first-century church is a total rejection of the tradition that characterizes her as the "sinful woman." There is no place in the canonical gospels where that association is made. There is no place in the noncanonical gospels where that association is made or implied. There is absolutely no reason to assume that Mary had been a harlot. In his commentary on Luke 8:1–3, Norval Geldenhuys wrote: "She is not to be identified with the sinful woman of Luke 7:37 (cf. Klosterman, in loc.). We nowhere read that being possessed by evil spirits had any connection with marked sinfulness."[5] It is also interesting to remember that Peter says to Jesus, "Depart from me for I am a sinful man" (Luke 5:9). Who concludes that Peter was a prostitute?

In an article in *Bible Review,* Jane Schaberg places the blame for the practice of identifying Mary of Magdala as a whore on male bias, "which fulfills the desire—or the need—to downgrade the Magdalene, as well as the desire to attach to female sexuality the notions of evil, repentance and mercy."[6] Prescinding from the polemical nature of that comment, which may be well taken, it is valid to operate out of the conviction that identifying Mary of Magdala as a sinful woman is not scriptural and should be abandoned. The important role played by Mary in the apocryphal gospels furnishes additional evidence against this identification.

It is also important to establish that Mary of Magdala cannot be identified with Mary of Bethany. The reasons are cogent. Mary of Bethany was clearly a Judean, while Mary of Magdala was just as obviously a Galilean. Mary of Bethany was of a contemplative nature (John 11:20, Luke 10:38–42), Mary of Magdala was an activist (Luke 8:1–3), and so on. Further evidence that Mary of Magdala was not the woman who washed Jesus' feet can be found in chapters 7 and 8 of Luke's gospel. The account of the woman who washed Jesus' feet occurs at the end of chapter 7 (Luke 7:36–50). Mary of Magdala is mentioned by name in the passage that follows immediately upon it. It seems unlikely that the same woman would be named in the second of two passages that follow each other while she remains unnamed in the first.

Neither Mark 14:3–9 nor Matthew 26:6–13 identifies as a sinner the woman who had washed Jesus' feet. The fourth gospel identifies that woman as Mary of Bethany at whose family residence the scene occurs. In Mark and Matthew's accounts, the emphasis is on the preparation of Jesus' body for burial, while in the fourth gospel the emphasis is on the waste which Judas discerns in the action (John 12:1–8). There are simply no grounds for identifying Mary of Magdala with Mary of Bethany or with the "sinful woman."

The excuse that is most often used for naming Mary of Magdala a sinful woman is found in the passage in Luke 8:2: "Mary, called the Magdalene, from whom seven devils had gone out." For people in the first century of the Christian era, the expression, "from whom seven devils had gone out," would have meant that she had been cured of a serious illness. As George Buttrick points out, the number seven would accentuate the seriousness of her condition or possibly its recurrent nature.[7]

Some scholars speculate that Luke 8:2 is a reference to immoral behavior and hence to Mary of Magdala as prostitute. This error can be traced to the early fourth century of the Christian era. It is found in the writings of Ephraim the Syrian, 306–373 CE.

> Mary by the oil showed forth the mystery of his mortality, who by his teaching mortified the concupiscence of her flesh. Thus, the sinful woman by the flood of her tears in full assurance was rewarded with remission of sins from beside his feet.[8]

This misidentification had achieved official standing by the time of Pope Gregory the Great, 540–604 CE. In a homily about Mary of Magdala he noted that she was the woman

> who, at this time with the other Mary, saw the Lord after his resurrection, and drawing near, embraced his feet. Lord, I ask, what hands are these that grasp your feet before my eyes? That woman, who was a sinner in society; those hands, which were stained with evil have touched his feet who is at the Father's right

hand above the angels. Let us consider, if we can, what might be the very heart of that heavenly devotion, and the woman who had been immersed in the depth of the abyss, through her own fault, was so cleansed through grace in a flight of love.[9]

Gregory's homilies led to an effort to construct "a coherent life story for this single Magdalen," says Mycoff.[10] This life story portrayed Mary of Magdala as a sinful woman and, in those days, that meant as a prostitute. As recently as 1988 Carole Straw wrote: "Mary Magdalene [was] inspired inwardly through the spirit of compunction to repent of her sins by the very one who received her tears and forgave her transgressions outwardly."[11] This false picture is still painted in spite of the fact that it is nonscriptural and, even, has no basis in the apocryphal writings through the first three centuries of the Christian era. There is much evidence that Mary of Magdala cannot and should not be identified as a sinful woman and, *a fortiori,* should not be associated with prostitution. The fact that she was thus portrayed indicates how readily, in those early centuries, such a falsehood could be perpetrated and perpetuated. Mary of Magdala is mentioned only in Luke 8:1-3 and in the crucifixion, burial and resurrection narratives. It is important to avoid reading her into any other part of the New Testament.

The main work of this book will be to study the crucifixion, burial and empty-tomb narratives in the canonical gospels. The stories will be examined to determine the relationship between Mary and the other women; the variations in the lists of names; those elements that are common to the three synoptic accounts; and those elements that are unique to each gospel. This process permits the separation of the traditional story from the redactional additions of the individual writers and the communities that commissioned the writing of the gospels. The study of these three-episode narratives will be undertaken primarily from a literary standpoint, although redaction and historical criticism will play important parts.

The fourth gospel will be examined separately for several reasons. The presence of Mary of Magdala in the crucifixion scene fulfills a very different purpose from that which it had in the synoptic gospels. The burial account in this gospel, which does not include Mary of Magdala or any other woman, stresses that Jesus' body was anointed with spices before burial. This changes the focus of the journey of Mary to the tomb. The first section of the fourth gospel's resurrection narrative, John 20:1–18, will be examined in detail as it sheds much light on the role of Mary of Magdala and may well be the earliest narrative of the risen Christ.

Some recent archeological, inscriptional and epigraphical findings will be examined in order to determine if any women achieved positions of rank or influence in Roman society, in Hellenistic circles or in Jewish society in the first century of the Christian era. These findings will answer the question: Could Mary of Magdala possibly have achieved an important leadership role in the early church? If other women were able to achieve places of importance in social, religious, economic and political situations, then it is possible that Mary of Magdala could have done so. Then the evidence available in the apocryphal literature will be examined to see if there are persistent themes or structures which might indicate something of the stature Mary of Magdala enjoyed in the Christian communities of the late first, second and third centuries. This will help in discerning what role Mary of Magdala really played in Jesus' time and in the postapostolic era.

CHAPTER 2

Scriptural Evidence

There is solid evidence that Mary of Magdala was a prominent leader in the early church. This becomes obvious through examination of the New Testament writings. Three considerations are important before beginning the exegesis of the texts wherein Mary of Magdala appears. The fact that her name does not appear in Paul's list of those to whom the risen Lord had appeared must be considered, as must the use of the terms "disciple," "apostle" and "the Twelve." The toponym (place name) "Mary, the woman of Magdala" will be studied to determine its importance in identifying this prominent woman.

In Paul's Writings

Mary of Magdala was important enough and prominent enough in the gospel communities that her name was retained in all the accounts of Jesus' crucifixion and resurrection. By contrast, there is no mention of Mary of Magdala or of any other woman in the "tradition" handed down by Paul in the first letter to the Corinthians. There are several reasons for the significant difference between Paul's statements and the gospel accounts. Paul writes:

> For I handed on to you as of first importance what I also received: that Christ died for our sins in accordance with the scriptures; that he was buried; that he was raised on the third day in accordance with the scriptures; that he appeared to

Kephas, then to the Twelve. After that, he appeared to more than five hundred brothers at once, most of whom are still living, though some have fallen asleep. After that he appeared to James, then to all the apostles. Last of all, as to one born abnormally, he appeared to me. (1 Cor 15:3–8)

Paul failed to mention an appearance of the risen Christ to Mary of Magdala or to any other woman. The most obvious reason for this difference between Paul's letter and the gospel accounts, and also the most difficult to refute, is the fact that the passage from First Corinthians is in the form of kerygma, a form structurally different from the appearance narratives in the gospels. Scholars have noted the differences between these two forms and some of the reasons for the differences. For example, Reginald Fuller notes that

> the appearances formed no part of the primitive kerygma or catechesis either in the form of lists or in the form of narratives. The earliest church did not prove the reality of the resurrection from the appearances. It simply affirmed it kerygmatically.[1]

Paul used a list of the appearances after the resurrection, but did not include stories about them. Evidently the names of women were associated with the appearances. Paul was employing a list to provide room to include himself as recipient of an appearance. Fuller suggests that this may have been the result of the necessity Paul felt to affirm his own status as apostle.[2]

The pre-Pauline tradition that Paul used in First Corinthians 15 came from the very earliest traditions about the Easter experience. Says Edward Lynn Bode:

> Thus allowing for the formulation of the tradition and its acceptance previous to the preaching of Paul at the mid-century in

Corinth, one has to conclude that the material stands in a very close relationship to the events described.[3]

Paul's concern was to publish and to proclaim, to announce openly that Christ had died, was buried, was raised and had appeared. He was not concerned with details of how, when, or where. Fuller explains:

> The meaning conveyed is invariably both a disclosure of Jesus as resurrected in the apocalyptic sense of the word, that is, as translated into eschatological existence, and a call of the recipient to a specific function in salvation history. In the case of the first three appearances (Cephas, the Twelve, and the 500+) this salvation-historical significance is concerned with the foundation of the church as eschatological community, while the later three appearances, those to James, to all the apostles, and to Paul, are concerned with the inauguration of the apostolic mission of the church beyond Jerusalem.[4]

The listing of the names of those the gospel tradition held to be recipients, then, was precluded in First Corinthians 15 by its very design, and even more so was the listing of the names of women who had been witnesses to the mystery of resurrection.

Another reason that Paul would not include the names of the women who witnessed to the resurrection is the fact that the lists of those to whom the risen Lord had appeared differ greatly in Pauline writings from those in the gospels. Paul mentions appearances to James and to 500-plus disciples. There is no record of either of these appearances in the gospels. The empty-tomb narratives, all four of them, are consistent in regard to the time when the discovery was made, the question about the stone being rolled back, the presence of angelic messengers, the mention of Galilee. These common points are so strong in the gospels that they must have been strong in the tradition. Paul used none of this material. There is no mention of an appearance to Peter alone in the gospel accounts even though Peter and the "other disciple whom Jesus loved" ran to the tomb and verified that it was empty. After that they returned home, eliminating themselves from the subsequent appearance to Mary of Magdala.

Paul's kerygmatic statement, a tradition that he had received, is clearly oriented toward the fact of resurrection and toward Paul's participation in the announcement of it. The gospel accounts just as clearly intend to stress the women, the specific time, the stone, the messengers and the commissioning of the women to carry the message. The purposes, forms, details are unique to each of the types, kerygma and empty-tomb narrative. If the exclusion of the women from Paul's writing would be seen as an indication that, historically, they were not witnesses to the resurrection, all of the other differences would also have to be considered.

There is no question that Paul wrote little or nothing of the details about the historical Jesus except that he was, indeed, a historical person. In Second Corinthians Paul wrote: "Consequently, from now on we regard no one according to the flesh; even if we once knew Christ according to the flesh, yet now we know him so no longer" (2 Cor 5:16). Paul's announced and consistent theme was "new creation" in which all people are joined "in Christ." He was almost totally silent on the matter of Jesus' life except for the important fact that he had been born of a woman: "But when the fullness of time had come, God sent his Son, born of a woman, born under the law" (Gal 4:4). While the reference is to the historical Jesus, the context is directed to the theme of the adoption of the whole race, "so that we might receive adoption" (Gal 4:5). Paul's direction here was the explanation that "Sonship is therefore a gift of the great time of redemption that has dawned in Christ," as Ridderbos points out.[5] Even when making this rare reference to the historical Jesus, it is clear that Paul's concern is with life in

Christ. If Paul were so loath to use the historical facts of Jesus' life, it is reasonable to expect that he would avoid them when speaking of the great mystery of resurrection.

Some writers have suggested that the list of those who had witnessed to the risen Christ, as listed by Paul, contains a polemic between the disciples of Paul and those of James.[6] It is not easy to dismiss this argument because there is so much evidence of a struggle between Peter and Mary of Magdala in the apocryphal gospels, or at least between their adherents. If Paul were recognizing an adversarial stance between Peter and James, it would only make sense not to muddy the waters with another conflict such as that which seems to have existed between Peter and Mary of Magdala.

Finally, there is the accusation that Paul was a misogynist and that this hatred or fear of women would have kept him from mentioning them as primary witnesses to resurrection. The accusation against Paul, in its most absolute form, can be obviated immediately by a simple reading of chapter 16 of Romans and of other texts where Paul referred with respect and gratitude to women who were his coworkers, heads of house churches, deacons and apostles. For example:

I commend to you Phoebe our sister, who is also a minister [Greek *diakonos*] of the church at Cenchreae. (Rom 16:1)

Greet Andronicus and Junia...they are prominent among the apostles. (Rom 16:7)

...Aquila and Prisca together with the church in their house. (1 Cor 16:19)

There is neither Jew nor Greek, there is neither slave nor free person, there is not male and female; for you are all one in Christ Jesus. (Gal 3:28)

There are some distinctions that must be made in the passages where Paul deals with women and women's issues because, although unity amid diversity is central to his understanding of human beings in relation to God, he is aware of everyday realities. He has no choice but to support some cultural and ethnic practices that had to be acknowledged in whole or in part; for example, the necessity of head coverings for women. Paul speaks strongly about equality in Christ, as in the passage from Galatians above. As he says, "one and the same Spirit produces all of these, distributing them individually to each person as he wishes" (1 Cor 12:11), and "so whoever is in Christ is a new creation" (2 Cor 5:17). Paul addresses all listeners as "saints" without specifying gender.

Paul was not a misogynist. He understood the realities of his time at the same time that he accorded women the acceptance and respect he believed they deserved as coworkers. He rejected anything that could be construed as limiting the power of the Spirit.

The Twelve, the Apostles, the Disciples

In order to define the leadership role that Mary of Magdala held in the first-century church, it is necessary to look at the various terms by which the gospels distinguish, or seem to distinguish, one group of followers from another. The terms "the Twelve," "apostle" and "disciple" are used of those who were with Jesus and who learned from him. Each of these designations has a unique meaning but it is misleading to regard them as absolute and to envision those who were with Jesus dividing themselves into groups according to such distinctions. The terms are literary devices, each with a specific quality designating differing aspects of the self-definition of the members of the earliest communities.

The expression "the Twelve" is used thirty times in the canonical gospels. It is employed in three types of context in these gospels:

eight times it is used to identify Judas as "one of the Twelve," and once it is used of Thomas in the same way; nine times it is used in the description of the formation of this group by Jesus, and the remaining uses deal with the designation of the group as those who had special instruction from Jesus. Since the designation "the Twelve" deals so often with identifying Judas as "one of the Twelve," and Thomas this way once, and the two other common uses of the term are also used of those who are called apostles, the specifying meaning of "the Twelve" would seem to be found in the references to Judas and to Thomas. The designation, "Judas, one of the Twelve," must have had its origin in the post-Easter community since it is so consistently applied to Judas and only in the post-Easter community could Judas have been known as the one who had betrayed Jesus.

The term "the Twelve" itself certainly carries a symbolic meaning. E. P. Sanders has written:

> What seems virtually certain is that the conception of "the Twelve" goes back to Jesus himself (though his closest companions at any given moment may not have consisted precisely of twelve men). His use of the conception "twelve" points toward his understanding of his own mission. He was engaged in a task that would include the restoration of Israel.[7]

The "Twelve" is a technical expression of covenant reality—it is a manner of speaking of the new community as "all Israel" that now lives in a new covenant. The number is a literary device, as the efforts of the writers to keep twelve persons around Jesus testify. However, the symbolism is clearly the important reality. Twelve is a symbolic number and its meaning is of the utmost importance. It points to the reappearance of the twelve tribes of Israel, "all Israel," as the new covenant reality. In this covenant reality Mary of Magdala and all women and men are included.

The term "apostle" is quite different. It appears nine times in the synoptic gospels and not at all in the fourth gospel. Three of the uses in the synoptic gospels describe the election of the "twelve who were also named apostles" (Matt 10:2, Mark 3:14, Luke 6:13), so the term "apostle" includes the idea of having been chosen for a specific group to receive special instruction from Jesus. Matthew uses the word only in this sense. Mark speaks of Jesus gathering apostles who had been sent out as "the twelve" after their first missionary endeavor. The remaining uses of the term "apostle" (six separate references) are found in the Lukan narrative. Only Luke refers to those brought to the last supper as apostles. Matthew and Mark designate them as "the Twelve." It is evident that the terms "apostle" and "the Twelve" were not clearly distinguished from each other. In the Lukan narrative particularly, the term "apostle" has to do with being sent out but it also carries other meanings. In the canonical gospels, the term "apostle" does not carry a clear, specific, unique meaning. "The Twelve" were considered apostles on one level while on the symbolic level the term included all of the new Israel.

In the examination of the empty-tomb narrative in the fourth gospel, it will be pointed out that Mary of Magdala's words, "I have seen the Lord" (John 20:18), qualify her as apostle according to Paul's use of the term. ("Am I not an apostle? Have I not seen Jesus our Lord?" Paul asks in First Corinthians 9:1.) In the Pauline sense, Mary of Magdala was an apostle. It would be erroneous to limit that designation to "apostle of the resurrection" unless in using the term it is recognized that to be an apostle of the resurrection is to be fully an apostle, that is, one sent out. The only other clear meaning of the term is to have been chosen and formed into a group to receive special instruction from Jesus. There is a great deal more reason to believe that Mary was part of such a group than that she was not.

The other designation common to the gospel texts is "disciple." There are seventy-nine uses of the verb "to follow" in the gospels and more than two hundred uses of the word "disciple." The terms are not used interchangeably but they seem to include all those who heard and believed in Jesus. Compared to thirty-nine uses of "the Twelve" and nine of "apostle," the dominance of the idea of discipleship is clear.

The term "disciple," as we read it in the gospels, is not gender-exclusive. *The Anchor Bible Dictionary* defines disciples as "people in the New Testament who stood in a special and intensive relationship with the earthly Jesus."[8] It goes on to say, admittedly with too much temerity, "In all probability women, too, belonged to these disciples."[9] Thus, that dictionary describes *disciples* as those who, having received a call, are able to break with the past and enter into a lifelong relationship with Jesus. Mary of Magdala received a call, in the garden on resurrection morning, if not before. Her lifelong relationship with Jesus is borne out by the gospels and the apocrypha. Luke mentions Mary among the women who were with Jesus and who provided for him and his other disciples out of their means. Mary's name heads the list of the women who were close by at the crucifixion, who were witnesses to the burial and who went out early to the tomb. Mary of Magdala was, without question, prominent among the disciples of Jesus. Possibly the inclusion of the names of other women in the synoptic accounts should signify to us that her relationship with Jesus was quite similar to that of many other women.

In terms, then, of the various designations used in the gospels, Mary of Magdala has no place among "the Twelve" if the term implies a group of human beings around Jesus. It certainly applies in its symbolic meaning as the New Israel, and she is certainly part of the "Twelve" who represent the New Israel, as were all of the disciples. She is truly "apostle" in the Pauline sense of the word and in the sense of having been sent out to proclaim the Good News of salvation. By any definition of the word, Mary of Magdala was a disciple of the Lord and was known to be so.

Mary, the Woman of Magdala

Mary of Magdala is mentioned by name in eleven incidents in the canonical gospels. Mary, the mother of Jesus, is the only woman whose name appears more frequently. It is significant that Mary of Magdala is always referred to by the toponym (place name) "Magdala"—in most instances, "Mary, the woman from Magdala" (*Maria ē Magdalēnē*).

Geography may have played an important role. Scholars tell us that

> for biblical writers place names conveyed meanings (or were expected to do so). Place names are usually transparent within the name-giving community, often reflecting physical aspects of the site and/or social, ideological and religious attitudes of the name-giving culture."[10]

The name Magdala refers to "Migdol," a port city on the western shore of the Sea of Galilee six kilometers northwest of Tiberias.[11] It is known to have been a fishing port, and possibly a center for woven goods in the first century BCE. According to Josephus, it was an important center for rebels during the Jewish Wars[12] if, as many scholars agree, Magdala was then known by the name Tarichaeae. Gauer writes: "Migdal (modern name for Magdala) recovered and became one of the centers of Jewish life in Galilee in the first centuries, CE."[13]

Avi-Yonah, the noted Jewish archeologist, asserts that, "his (Jesus') main activity was, however, in and around Capernaum, 'his city.' Magdala was the home of Mary of Magdala and Bethsaida whence came the apostles Peter, Andrew and Philip."[14] He states further that the locations of Capernaum and Magdala are definitely identified.[15] From the welter of archeological and historical data, it is safe to assume that Magdala was a significant town with a well-established fishing trade and probably also a weaving trade. There is significant evidence that it came back to life after the devastation of the Jewish Wars.

Although none of this material can be called upon to establish definite connections with the Mary of Magdala whose name appears in the canonical gospels, it provides some background for consideration of the absolute, unfailing identification of this woman as "the woman from Magdala." It is just possible that Magdala's proximity to Capernaum, Mary's origin from the same area as Peter's, Andrew's and Philip's, and the fact that the town was known to have existed during the time of the writing of the canonical gospels may yet shed some light on the role of Mary of Magdala in the early church.

In the canonical gospels, Mary of Magdala is always referred to by the geographical place name. In these same gospels there are twenty-seven references to other persons using geographical names. These references are found in six different forms, each of which seems to have a slightly different nuance. In five places the expressions "was called," or "by name" are used as in "Then one of the Twelve, who was called Judas Iscariot..." (Matt 26:14). These two expressions seem to associate the person with the place. The person is identified by place to distinguish him or her from another person with the same name. It might also be that the identification is not absolutely certain.

In five other instances in the canonical gospels, a person is associated with a place by use of the preposition *apo* (from), as in "Lazarus from Bethany" (John 11:1) and "Joseph from Arimathea" (Mark 15:43). The use of the prepositional phrase is to place some distance between the person and the place. Joseph has "come out" or "gone out" of Arimathea. There is a sense of a past relationship that is being used for purposes of identification.

Four times Judas Iscariot is mentioned by the proper name with the toponym in apposition but without an article, *Ioudan 'Iskarioth.* This occurs in Mark 3:19, Mark 14:10, Luke 6:16 and, with slight variation, in John 13:2: "The devil had already induced Judas, son of Simon the Iscariot...." The same form, proper noun and toponym, without an article, is used in Mark 15:21 referring to "Simon the Canaanite" (*Simona Kurenaion*). This is the normal form used both in classical Greek and in New Testament Greek. Moulton describes it:

> But in classical Greek, names of towns do not require the article and even the anaphoric use is sometimes merely a device to avoid a hiatus: NT follows the rule and has the article only for a special reason.[16]

The omission of the article before a place name in a construction that identifies a person was the normal practice. When an article was used, some special purpose was being served.

Another grammatical form for identifying a person by a place name is found in Mark 14:67, when the young girl accuses Peter of having been with Jesus, "You also were with the Nazarene, Jesus" (*su meta tou Nazarenou, estha tou, 'Iesou*). Mark consistently includes the article with the name of Jesus as he does here. The pronoun, "You," is followed by the preposition "with" (*meta*) and two genitive constructions, "Nazareth" (*tou Nazarenou*) and "Jesus" (*tou 'Iesou*). This establishes a relationship between Peter and Jesus based on the place name—it is the man from Nazareth with whom Peter has been associating. The reversal of word order, "the Nazarene, Jesus," stresses Jesus' origin rather than his person. It should be noted that the word used for Nazareth here is *Nazarenos* which always refers to an inhabitant of Nazareth. The other form, *Nazoraiou,* may mean either an inhabitant of Nazareth or a member of the Nazirite sect. Mark's meaning is clear: Jesus was an inhabitant of Nazareth.

Luke uses yet another form for identifying by a place name. An unclean spirit calls out, "What have you to do with us, Jesus of Nazareth?" (Luke 4:34). The demon addresses himself directly to Jesus, hence the vocative case. In Mark 14:67 and in Luke 4:34, the geographical reference is intended to identify the person through association with a place name, thereby distinguishing him from any other person with the same name.

Excluding the references to Mary of Magdala, there are nine places in the canonical gospels where the Greek construction— proper noun + definite article + geographical name—is used. These are:

Matthew 10:4 "Simon the Canaanite"
Mark 3:18 "Simon the Canaanite"
Luke 4:27 "Namaan the Syrian"
Matthew 26:69 "Jesus the Galilean"
Matthew 26:71 "Jesus the Nazarean"
Mark 10:47 "Jesus the Nazarean"
Luke 18:37 "Jesus the Nazarean"
John 18:5 "Jesus the Nazarean"
John 19:15 "Jesus the Nazarean"

Only three uses of this form—proper noun + definite article + geographical name—refer to persons other than Jesus. Simon and Namaan are identifiable as having come from a specific location, in each case an area rather than a city or village. In all of the other appearances of this form, Jesus is identified as the one from

Nazareth, or in one case as from Galilee. As Moulton described it, the inclusion of the definite article indicates that a special reason exists for making this identification in this manner. Clearly, Jesus is to be regarded as special. The Blass-De Brunner text supports the thesis that the presence of the definite article in this construction indicates some special distinction.[17] The appositive structure is described: "appositives with proper names take the article if a well-known person is to be distinguished from others of the same name."[18] Jesus is frequently described by a geographical place name in an appositive structure using a definite article for the obvious purpose of acknowledging his importance.

This makes even more significant the fact that Mary of Magdala is almost without exception referred to by the same grammatical form. She is mentioned nine times in the formula proper noun + definite article + geographical name, and twice in very minor variations of this form. In Luke 8:2 is found, "Mary, called Magdalene." The only other place in Luke where Mary is referred to by name is in 24:10, which reads, "Mary Magdalene." In Greek, the definite article is retained even though the word order is reversed. Moulton attempts to explain why the Lukan author is the only gospel writer to change the form by which Mary of Magdala was identified. The proper noun usually comes first: "Hence [the sixth-century New Testament manuscript] D corrects '*ē Magdalēnē Maria*' to '*Maria ē Magdalēnē.*'"[19] Moulton goes on to assert that the Lukan author seems to wish to single Mary out for special attention because the omission of the verb "to be" was used in some manuscripts to improve the syntax while "the reading '*en de*' preserved in [the ninth-century New Testament manuscript] K II et al. singles out Mary Magdalene for special attention."[20] So the variation in the form in Luke is an effort to increase the importance assigned to Mary of Magdala rather than simply to provide an alternative form to the distinctive form *"Maria ē Magdalēnē."* The New Testament texts use the form *"Maria ē Magdalēnē"* with unusual consistency.

Mary of Magdala is mentioned three times in the Matthean narrative: once in the crucifixion scene, once at the burial and once at the empty tomb. All three references employ the same form: proper name + definite article + geographical name. A slight variation occurs in the word "Maria" which becomes "Mariam" in two of these references. "Maria" is classified as indeclinable and the spelling variation is not known to mean anything, represented both as Mariam and Maria.[21] For all practical purposes, the three references in the Matthean gospel are identical.

The three references in the Markan gospel are even more precise: "Among them were Mary Magdalene" (Mark 15:40), "Mary Magdalene and Mary the mother of Joses" (Mark 15:47) and "When the Sabbath was over, Mary Magdalene..." (Mark 16:1). The same form in Greek, *Maria ē Magdalēnē,* is used in all three.

The Johannine author uses that same form in three references: "Standing by the cross of Jesus were his mother and his mother's sister, Mary the wife of Clopas, and Mary of Magdala" (John 19:25); "On the first day of the week, Mary of Magdala came to the tomb..." (John 20:1) and "Mary of Magdala went and announced to the disciples..." (John 20:18). The evidence is clear that the form used to identify this particular disciple of Jesus was already encapsulated in a technical term by the time the gospels were written. Her name was well enough established for the gospel writers to use it consistently in identifying her and in causing at least one scribe to introduce an alternate wording that enhances its importance.

This evidence can only lead to the conclusion that "Mary, the woman from Magdala," was the recognized title of this woman at the time the canonical gospels were written. The reason for the precision and the common use of the title must be that it was the recognized way of referring to this woman. The name had become a technical appellation for the woman who had stood by the cross of Jesus, who had witnessed his burial and who had played a primary role in the discernment of resurrection. Everything about this identification bespeaks a person who was recognizable to most members of the four gospel communities, who was known to have been a disciple of Jesus and who played a major role in the early church.

Mary of Magdala was so prominent in the early church that it was impossible to omit her name from the texts and equally impossible to change the form of the identifying phrase by which she was known. The frequency and consistency with which this form is used signifies widespread and accepted usage. The prominence of the form also indicates that the basic narratives of crucifixion, burial and resurrection contained a personal name, in a specific formulation, which could neither be minimalized nor omitted. Mary of Magdala was indeed a leader and apostle in the early church. No other position is ascribed to her.

CHAPTER 3

Mary of Magdala in Mark and Matthew

Mary of Magdala is clearly a major figure in the synoptic accounts of the crucifixion, burial and empty-tomb events. Her name appears three times in each of the Markan and Matthean accounts. She is mentioned by name early in Luke's account in a pericope where that author describes a group of women disciples who provided for Jesus and his other disciples out of their own financial resources (Luke 8:1–3). She is referred to among the "women who had followed him from Galilee" (Luke 23:49 and 23:55) and again in the empty-tomb narrative (Luke 24:10). Mary of Magdala is the only woman mentioned by name in all three synoptic empty-tomb narratives. There are significant reasons for believing that the account that has Mary of Magdala going alone to the tomb in the twentieth chapter of the fourth gospel is from the earliest traditions and that the synoptic accounts were based upon it, directly or indirectly.

There has been a vast amount of scholarly discussion of the relationship which does, or does not, exist between the Passion accounts and the empty-tomb narratives. Reginald Fuller writes, "...the empty tomb story is a later legend, introduced by Mark for the first time into the narrative."[1] John Alsup is even more precise, "Here, as there, inner criteria support the supposition that the tomb story and the Passion narrative were not originally an organic unity."[2] In the Anchor Bible commentary *Mark,* C. S. Mann says that "the narrative of the burial in Mark belongs to the Passion tradition and is ancient. The visit to the tomb is legendary."[3] There is a fair distribution of the opinion among contemporary scholars that the empty-tomb narratives are later additions to the gospel narratives and are separate from the Passion accounts.

On the other hand, there are many serious studies concluding that the three accounts—the crucifixion, the burial and the visit to the tomb—form a literary and narrative unity. William L. Craig notes Rudolf Pesch's analysis: "Pesch explains that the empty tomb story is no independent pericope, but is bound up with the Passion story and the immediate context."[4] Craig continues with a series of reasons why he believes the three stories form one unity. He cites narrative sequence, the time references and verbal and syntactic indicators. Norman Perrin agrees: "It will be evident by now that for me the resurrection narrative in Mark is the threefold narrative concerning the women at the cross, the burial and the empty tomb."[5]

Once we assume that the synoptic authors wrote a unified sequence that includes empty-tomb narratives, examination of the three texts becomes a tool for finding the objectives behind the portrayal of the women in the Passion-resurrection narratives, especially the role of Mary of Magdala. There are many questions to be raised about these stories. For example, what role did women play in the crucifixion scene? Why do they plan to anoint Jesus' body after the Sabbath, or do they? Why is Mary of Magdala always mentioned first and why is her name the only one that appears in every empty-tomb narrative? The answers to these questions provide keys to understanding the role of Mary of Magdala in the unfolding drama of the end of Jesus' earthly existence.

Mark

In the Markan narrative, the stories of the crucifixion, burial and resurrection are connected by a running narrative sequence. Some of the methods by which the author achieves this are the time references, the theme of lack of understanding and the role of the women led by Mary of Magdala.

In Mark, each of the three stories begins with a careful mention of the time the event occurred. The account of Jesus' death begins with the words, "At noon darkness came over the whole land until three in the afternoon" (Mark 15:33). The burial scene begins with the time designation, "When it was already evening" (Mark 15:42), and the empty-tomb narrative begins with the words, "When the Sabbath was over" (Mark 16:1). The effect of this precision is to establish a three-day sequence with an orderly progression from one event to the next. The fact that the final scene occurs on the third day is, of course, a traditional reference both in the Hebrew scriptures (Hosea 6:1-2, Genesis 42:18 and so forth) and in the cult of the "dying and rising fertility gods; at least in Babylonia the re-awakening began on the third day."[6]

The Markan theme of disbelief also helps in unifying the three events. The author has consistently portrayed a lack of understanding about Jesus shown by those who surround him. Jesus' family and neighbors are said to have been lacking in faith (Mark 3:31-35 and 6:1-6). No one of the group of Jesus' family and friends reappears in Mark's account after the strong words, "He was not able to perform any mighty deeds there, apart from curing a few sick people by laying his hands on them. He was amazed at their lack of faith" (Mark 6:5-6). At chapter 14:50, the disciples all leave him and flee. The Jewish officials had opposed Jesus from the very beginning of his ministry (Mark 3:6). Only Mary of Magdala and the other women are present for the final events and even they flee "seized with trembling and bewilderment" from the empty tomb (Mark 16:8). Misunderstanding and lack of faith play a major role in the Markan narrative.

Jesus experiences a very painful sense of abandonment in the Markan crucifixion scene. In the words of Psalm 22, he cries out to know why even God has forsaken him, "My God, my God, why have you forsaken me?" (Mark 15:34). While bystanders mock him, the Roman centurion proclaims him Son of God and the women stand at a distance and watch. At the burial scene, the women watch "where he was laid" (Mark 15:47). Finally, the women come to the empty tomb with three concerns each of which is ill-advised or unnecessary. In the empty-tomb scene, the women become part of the pattern Mark has established. Mark refers frequently to those who had good reason to know who Jesus is yet do not understand him. At the same time, like the Roman centurion who had little or no reason to know who Jesus is, the women do have some insight into his identity. The women run off and say nothing to anyone "for they were afraid" (Mark 16:8). They do not understand but they are willing to be there, to attempt to render a final service. Quite rightly the Markan redactor awards them pride of place.

The Markan inclusion of the lists of women at the three final events is another device for attaining a unified sequence. Mary of Magdala heads the list in each instance. She and the women with her have the function of witnessing the death, knowing where the body was buried and returning to the tomb on the third day. Mary of Magdala is always mentioned first and Mary, the mother of James and Joses, is also mentioned in all three accounts with minor variations in the names of her sons. Salome, who is mentioned only here in the entire New Testament, is named in the crucifixion scene and at the empty tomb. The variations in the lists make it even more noteworthy that Mary of Magdala is consistently mentioned first. For this type of text and for this period of writing, such consistency is most unusual. The Markan redactor, for example, often feels free to alter details in order to emphasize his point as he does in the geographical references in chapter 3:7 and in the description of the women who witness the crucifixion. The lists of the names of the women contribute significantly to the unity of the three passages. They also stress the primacy of Mary of Magdala and the importance of the women witnesses.

Some irony is built up by the statement about Jesus' disciples that "they all left him and fled," in Mark 14:50. The cowardly defection of the male disciples contrasts sharply with the calm presence of the women throughout the events of Jesus' final hours. The absence of the male disciples from the crucifixion scene is so humiliating and unpleasant to contemplate that some historical reality must lie behind it. Such a cowardly action would hardly have been invented in the early church. All three of the synoptic gospels place women, but not men, at the crucifixion, burial and empty tomb.

Mark 15:40–41 reads:

> There were also women looking on from a distance. Among them were Mary Magdalene, Mary the mother of the younger James and of Joses, and Salome. These women had followed him when he was in Galilee and ministered to him. There were also many other women who had come up with him to Jerusalem.

"There were also women...." The "also" construction (*kai*) indicates that the women were not alone at the place of crucifixion. There were mocking bystanders and the Roman centurion also present along with the women disciples. They were standing a distance away in three distinct groups. Mary of Magdala, Mary the mother of James and Joses and Salome[7] form one group as the Markan author describes the scene. Also present were more women who had "also" come with Jesus from Galilee. The third group was comprised of "other women" who had come up with him to Jerusalem. This presents a fairly sizable contingent of women who were both loyal enough and courageous enough to stand nearby at the time of the death of Jesus.

In Mark 15:40 and 41, the narrator voice is detached and fully objective. There is neither praise nor blame, simply the narration of facts. The style is, in fact, reportorial. The only adjectives which occur in these verses, whose obvious intent is to describe the women observers, are "younger" applied to one of Mary's sons and "many other" used to give a sense of the size of the group of women followers. Those who are present are mentioned only in their role as witnesses and no other information is given about them. It would be logical to assume that some Roman official would be present at an execution, but this centurion, who has not been mentioned before this moment, makes the seminal proclamation of who Jesus is. He is not seen or heard again. In like manner, the groups of women are enumerated with some care, their role as watchers and as disciples is established, but no comment is made on the motives for their presence. Neither fear, nor anxiety, nor devotion, nor any other emotion is described. The narrator's concern is single-mindedly on Jesus and on the onlookers only in their relation to Jesus. He is not interested in other details, not even to praise the few women disciples who had courage enough to be present.

The account of the burial is even less embellished. "Mary Magdalene and Mary the mother of Joses watched where he was laid" (Mark 15:47). Again the writer has only one interest, to establish the fact that the women knew where Jesus' body had been placed. They will be the reliable witnesses to the location of the tomb. No hint is given about how they came to be there, whether they assisted Joseph in the preparation of the body for burial, or what their reactions were to the burial. They are just there. The Markan author simply records their presence and hints of the fact that they could find their way back to this tomb later if opportunity should arise.

One method of establishing unity in a work is to recognize that no incidents could be excised from the text without changing it radically. All three of the incidents in which the women are present are essential to the unfolding narrative—none could be omitted without radically changing the whole. It should be noted that, among those somehow committed to Jesus, only the women were witnesses to the two proclamations—that of the Roman centurion: "Truly this man was the Son of God" (Mark 15:39), and the later proclamation that he had risen: "He has been raised; he is not here" (Mark 16:6). Not only are the incidents important to the unity of the narrative but the women are vital to it also as they alone have heard the two important proclamations.

All three of the synoptic gospels relate the narrative of the events at the empty tomb in an account that indicates the likelihood of a strong traditional story underlying them. The question of the order of composition of these narratives remains cloudy but some consensus is emerging that "there was a pre-Markan passion, burial and resurrection tradition."[8] William Craig cites Rudolf Pesch, Maurits Sabbe, Vincent Taylor and Johannes Gnilka in support of this position. The all but unsolvable nature of the classic "synoptic problem" given the choice between the Two-Document Hypothesis and the Greisbach hypothesis makes the multiple source hypothesis of M. E. Boismard suggestive of an important new direction.[9] In reviewing the Boismard work, E. P. Sanders concludes: "The reviewer, further, shares Boismard's view that we have reached the stage at which complex solutions to the synoptic problem should be considered."[10] The acceptance of a hypothesis of a multiple tradition that predates any of the written gospels enables the reader to examine the texts as they are, without feeling bound to trace the influence of Mark upon Matthew or of Matthew upon Mark. Those elements that are found in all of the empty-tomb narratives may be considered part of the preredactional tradition, while those that are unique to one of the texts may provide an insight into the theological or practical presuppositions of the community that formulated that particular narrative.

Mark and Matthew

Each of the empty-tomb narratives adds to the picture of Mary of Magdala according to that particular community's understanding of her. It is important to begin by noting how much of the story is common to all of them. The empty-tomb stories in Mark and Matthew are strikingly similar. Matthew sets the time with the words, "After the Sabbath" (Matt 28:1), while Mark begins, "When the Sabbath was over" (Mark 16:1).

The Matthean author is concerned to show that the Sabbath rest had been completed before the women set out and the Markan author stresses that point even more forcefully. There might have been several reasons for the precision with which the time is described. Perhaps it was important to point out that the women were respectful of Jewish observance, or the "third day" reference may have needed emphasis. Certainly there was an effort to include a connotation of new creation beginning on the first day of the week.

Both Matthew and Mark have an added reference to the time involved: "as the first day of the week was dawning" (Matt 28:1), and "very early when the sun had risen, on the first day of the week" (Mark 16:2). The phrases vary only slightly and seem to be adding to the original observation that the Sabbath rest had not been violated, that a sense of urgency existed, that there was considerable danger involved, and that the action required a great deal of devotion and love from those who had stood by the cross (Matt 27:55-56; Mark 15:40-41) and had witnessed the burial (Matt 27:61, Mark 15:47).

The Matthean account differs from the Markan in describing the reason for the women's visit to the tomb. In Matthew, they go "to see the tomb" (Matt 28:1); in Mark's account, they "bought spices so that they might go and anoint him" (Mark 16:1). Two difficulties exist in reading the account as Mark proposed it. Jesus had stated that the woman at Bethany had anointed his body for burial (Mark 14:8) and in the burial story, Joseph of Arimathea seems to have taken great care to buy a linen cloth, remove the body from the cross, wrap it in the linen cloth and lay it in the tomb. These descriptions led Reginald Fuller to conclude that Joseph of Arimathea had completed the burial rites and that, therefore, "the empty tomb story is a later legend, introduced by Mark for the first time into the narrative."[11] It may well be that the second difficulty is only apparent since Joseph would have to have acted with great dispatch to go to Pilate, obtain permission to bury Jesus, return to the scene of crucifixion, remove the body from the cross, wrap it and lay it in the tomb, all before sundown. It seems quite possible that he would not have had time to anoint the body and that the women who were sitting nearby knew this. Perhaps the very awkwardness apparent when the attempt is made to historicize the details makes this apparent difficulty irrelevant. The Markan redactor chose to portray Mary of Magdala and the other women coming to the tomb early on the day after the Sabbath for the expressed purpose of anointing Jesus' body for burial. The Matthean redactor chose to describe them simply as those who went out to see.

The variations in the names of the women who accompanied Mary stress the importance of the one whose name is always there and is always first. "Mary, the mother of James" is listed in both

Mark and Luke. The unknown Salome appears in Mark but in Luke the third woman is named Joanna. These names probably relate to some tradition in the early communities but the ease with which they are commingled and the precision with which Mary of Magdala stands out separates her unquestioned role from the shifting roles of the other women. It should be noted again that the Greek of Mary's name is identical in all references in Matthew and Mark. In Luke the phrase is the same except for the word order. Mary's name had clearly settled into what must be recognized as a well-known topographical designation by the time of the writing of the gospels. The gospel writers exercised considerable latitude in listing the names of her companions.

In the Markan narrative, two or three women go to anoint the body of Jesus. The Markan redactor has consistently portrayed the human companions and acquaintances of Jesus as those who do not understand Jesus or his mission.[12] In Mark's final scene, the women go out with three concerns, all of them without foundation. They go out to find the body of Jesus ("he is not here," Mark 16:6); they wish to anoint the body for burial but it had already been anointed; they are worried about rolling back the stone and it has already been rolled away (Mark 16:1–4). Mark's picture of the women, and therefore of Mary of Magdala, is one of failure to understand about Jesus even though they are in the process of performing an act of devotion which requires no little courage. Mary and her companions are the last in this gospel to fail to understand who Jesus is. The Jewish officials, Jesus' family and neighbors, his disciples have all failed to understand before the women, in a similar manner, fail to understand the full impact of the events. The enigmatic ending of this gospel, "They said nothing to anyone, for they were afraid" (Mark 16:8), completes the theme of human misunderstanding which pervades Mark. Mary of Magdala is the leader of a group of faithful women who desire to perform the rituals of Jewish burial that had been denied to Jesus because of the beginning of the Sabbath rest. Her lack of understanding in common with that of her companions is part of the redactional emphasis of the Markan gospel, "They said nothing to anyone for they were afraid" (Mark 16:8). It is the final forceful statement of that emphasis.

Matthew

> There were many women there, looking on from a distance, who had followed Jesus from Galilee, ministering to him. Among them were Mary Magdalene and Mary the mother of James and Joseph, and the mother of the sons of Zebedee. (Matt 27:55–56)

The Matthean author allows breaks in the narrative sequence when the women are mentioned in the crucifixion and burial scenes. This is a significant departure from the picture presented in the Lukan account. In Luke, the women are included in a large group of observers of Jesus' death. The group is comprised of the Roman centurion, the spectacle-seekers, Jesus' acquaintances, and the women. So, the women are part of a large cast who witness and fulfill various functions. In the Markan account, the women are the only observers present with the centurion—dramatizing Mark's motif of abandonment. In Matthew's account, the women at the crucifixion scene have no such group identification. They are inserted after the description of the apocalyptic signs (Matt 27:51–53) and the proclamation by the centurion. No connection is established between the women who are looking on: they are suddenly there. They are "looking on" (*theorousai*). In the empty-tomb narrative they are described as coming "to see the tomb." Again, the verb is a form of *theoreo* (Matt 28:1). But the angel tells them to go to the disciples and tell them that they will "see" (*opsesthe*) him in Galilee (Matt 28:7). They are told this again by Jesus: "Tell my brothers to

go to Galilee, and there they will see me" (*opsontai*) (Matt 28:10).
When the women see the tomb and when they are looking on, the
verb *theoreo* is used because sense perception is involved. When
the promise is made that the disciples will see him in Galilee, the
verb changes to forms of *horao* which may or may not involve sense
perception. The same pattern occurs in Mark and in the fourth
gospel.

The narrative sequence in the Matthean empty-tomb narrative
moves from the journey of the women to the tomb, to a description
of apocalyptic signs in Matthew 28:2–3, to the vision of the angel
sending the women to the disciples. Then Jesus appears to the
women disciples for the same purpose. It is easy to lose sight of the
women in the amazing portents and in the obvious emphasis on
delivering the message that the disciples will see Jesus in Galilee.
The verb *horao* had appeared in the Beatitudes—"Blessed are the
clean of heart for they shall see God" (Matt 5:8)—and when Judas
attempts to remit his sin by returning and confessing to the high
priests. They tell him: "Look to it yourself" (Matt 27:4). A form of the
same verb is used in Matthew's transfiguration narrative when
Jesus forbids Peter, James and John to tell anyone about what they
have seen (Matt 17:9). It is most often used with the sense of seeing,
without a direct object. The use of this verb, when the women are
twice told to tell the disciples that they will see Jesus in Galilee,
stresses the role of the women as witnesses to the crucifixion, burial and resurrection that is the primary emphasis of the Matthean
gospel narrative.

The portrayal in the Matthean narrative of women who at first
are looking and may be thought to be totally passive observers
changes radically when they assume the role of evangelists. This
resonates with the emphasis in the fourth gospel when Mary goes
to the other disciples and says simply, "I have seen the Lord" (John

20:18). In all of the empty-tomb narratives, Mary of Magdala leads the women in the dissemination of the message of resurrection.

In the burial scene in Matthew's gospel, the first verb is singular so Matthew 27:61 is translated from the Greek: "And she was there, Mary of Magdala...." There is difficulty with agreement since two women are named but the presence of the singular verb in the Greek—in a passage which in other aspects echoes the empty-tomb narrative of the fourth gospel—at least hints at the possibility that, in a pre-redactional story, Mary of Magdala was the first and only witness to the fact of resurrection.

The Matthean account differs from the Markan account of the event at the empty tomb because the theme of disbelief is absent in Matthew and the apocalyptic elements are missing from Mark. Because the two accounts are so similar, the differences become significant. Matthew's women leave the tomb "fearful yet overjoyed" (Matt 28:8) and run to tell the disciples. Unlike the parallel account in Mark, they had not been concerned about rolling away the stone, nor, it seems, had they come to anoint the body. This simplicity of detail strengthens the emphasis of the Matthean author that Mary of Magdala, and possibly another Mary, were important witnesses to the crucifixion, to the burial and to the empty tomb and resurrection.

The appearance narrative in Matthew is completely redactional (Matt 28:9–10). It even jars a bit by its departure from the Markan account with which, otherwise, it is in so much harmony. Jesus meets the women as they are returning from the tomb—an incident that bears strong resemblance to the encounter of Mary with Jesus in the fourth gospel. In John 20:14, Mary "turned" from the tomb; in Matthew's account the women depart quickly. In Matthew, "Jesus said to them..." (Matt 28:10) and in John, "Jesus said to her" (John 20:15). In both cases the absence of any descriptive details strengthens the encounter nature of the story. In Matthew, the women embrace the feet of Jesus; in the fourth gospel, Mary is told to stop clinging to him. The likenesses in the patterns of the appearance stories emphasize the significant difference between them.

In Matthew, the appearance is to two women but the verb problem, already noted, leaves open the possibility that the appearance in Matthew originally was an appearance to Mary of Magdala alone. And, in the difference between the women who take hold of his feet and worship him and Mary of Magdala who is told to stop clinging to him, can be found redactional emphases which create a significant difference between the two recountings of the same detail. Matthew is attempting to describe a joyful scene with recognition of the risen Christ that is immediate and unlimited. The fourth gospel portrayal, at this point, is concerned with the coming ascension. There seems to be an effort to distinguish between the Jesus of Nazareth whom Mary loved and the risen Christ of the ascension. Matthew has no such distinction. In both accounts, the action centers around Mary of Magdala.

In the Matthean account there is an emphasis on the joy of the discovery, on avoiding fear, and on sending the disciples to Galilee where they will see Jesus. In the fourth gospel the emphasis is on Mary in her relationship to Jesus, on the fact that he is going to ascend to the Father, and that Mary is to carry the message of resurrection to the disciples. Even with these redactional differences, Mary's role remains constant: she is the messenger and she is the one who understands who this risen Jesus is. She mediates the message of resurrection to the rest of the disciples. In Matthew's account, the second woman, possibly placed there simply to make the witness plural, is not described. She is simply "the other Mary" (Matt 28:1). Given the proliferation of Marys in the later gospels, this is a very vague description of the woman. The focus remains on Mary of Magdala.

CHAPTER 4

Mary of Magdala in Luke

The presentation of Mary of Magdala and her companions is markedly different in the Lukan account from the portrayals in Matthew and Mark. Luke mentions the women early in the course of the public life of Jesus; there is no such reference in Mark and Matthew, where it is mentioned only belatedly that some women disciples had been with Jesus while he ministered in Galilee. The Lukan narrative recounts:

> Afterward he journeyed from one town and village to another, preaching and proclaiming the good news of the kingdom of God. Accompanying him were the Twelve and some women who had been cured of evil spirits and infirmities, Mary, called Magdalene, from whom seven demons had gone out, Joanna, the wife of Herod's steward Chuza, Susanna, and many others who provided for them out of their resources. (Luke 8:1–3)

These women appear again at the crucifixion scene: "But all his acquaintances stood at a distance, including the women who had followed him from Galilee and saw these events" (Luke 23:49). In common with Matthew and Mark, the women are present at the burial scene: "The women who had come from Galilee with him followed behind..." (Luke 23:55). These are not the women with the same names as those mentioned in chapter 8. Joanna is named in both but Susanna is not included in the empty-tomb scene. In that narrative—in addition to Mary of Magdala and Joanna—the

49

woman present is "Mary the mother of James" (Luke 24:10). Since Mary, the mother of James, is mentioned by both Mark and Matthew, the name evidently was strong in the tradition. Susanna may be assumed to have been among the other women who accompanied Jesus.

There are more women in Luke's gospel than in any of the other gospels; there are more women named in Luke's gospel than in any other gospel; there are more women who lack names in Luke's gospel than in any other gospel. The list of those who are named includes Mary, Elizabeth, Anna, Mary of Magdala, Joanna, Susanna, Martha, Mary and Mary the mother of James. Those whom Luke introduces but does not name (or whose names were dropped) include the widow of Naim, the "sinful woman," Peter's mother-in-law, the "other women" who saw to Jesus' needs, the maid who accuses Peter, Jairus's daughter, the woman with a hemorrhage, the crippled woman, the women who call out "blessed is the womb that bore you," the poor widow, and possibly the unnamed disciple on the road to Emmaus. In addition, women are the actors in the parable of the lost coin and that of the persistent widow. For that age and that milieu, this is an impressive list. Robert J. Karris presents a fine summary of the Lukan presentation of women in four key points:

    a. Jesus goes against the mores of his time and associates freely with women, an "outcast" class.
    b. Jesus respects their full dignity.
    c. They are his most faithful followers.
    d. They seem to have played an important role in this church of Luke's time.[1]

This portrayal of women is part of the Lukan theme of the universality of salvation. Jesus came for all human beings. It is quite likely that this gospel gives a more realistic picture of the church in gospel times than the allegedly historical descriptions of that time that often depict a totally subordinate role for all women.

Luke 8:1–3

Near the beginning of Jesus' mission to Galilee, the Lukan author introduces a group of followers that includes "the Twelve" as well as many women. This author tends to identify "the Twelve" with the apostles.[2] The passage is unique to Luke but knowledge of women who ministered to Jesus and to his disciples in Galilee is also mentioned by Matthew and Mark: "These women had followed him when he was in Galilee and ministered to him" (Mark 15:41 and the parallel account in Matt 27:55). Many have noted that a favorite device in the Lukan narrative is the "twinning" of incidents dealing with female and male disciples. For example, both Simeon and Anna greet Mary as she presents Jesus in the temple (Luke 2:25–38); the cure of Peter's mother-in-law follows immediately upon the cure of the demoniac (Luke 4:31–39), and the parable of the Good Samaritan is followed by the story of Martha and Mary (Luke 10:29–42). The literary device employed here and elsewhere in Luke has the effect of making the term "disciple" gender-inclusive. A disciple is one who learns from or about Jesus, whether he or she is a man, woman or child.

There are four Lukan passages that refer to Mary of Magdala (Luke 8:1–3; 23:49; 23:55–56; 24:10–11). The passage found in Luke 8:1–3 is in the summary form which this author employs regularly (Luke 4:43; 4:40–41; 6:17–19 and so forth). In this gospel, summaries serve several purposes: they may mark a break in the narrative, that is, mark the end of one section and the beginning of a new one. Or they may provide the setting for some change in the narrative sequence, or introduce material not directly relating to the preceding text. In this instance (Luke 8:1–3), the summary seems to provide a generic description of an itinerant preacher and his followers, with the specific purpose of describing that group as both male and female. The style of the passage is distinctly Lukan in that the purpose of the segment is made very clear but the details are not clearly etched. The setting is vague, "from one town and village to another" (Luke 8:1) and the journey is not defined as to origin or destination. The journey is an essential part of identifying the itinerant preacher of the day with a group of followers of mixed sex, unusual as that was in Palestine in the first century CE

The first three verses of chapter 8 are clearly redactional. Fitzmyer cites several examples of specifically Lukan words and phrases. He lists: *kai egeneto, Kai autos, asthenxes, diodeuen, Euangelizomenos,* and *asthenia.*[3] In addition, there are details which echo the description of ministry in Luke's fourth chapter, especially verse 43, "To the other towns also I must proclaim the good news of the kingdom of God." And again in Luke 16:16, "The law and the prophets lasted until John; but from then on the kingdom of God is proclaimed." And Acts 8:12, "but once they began to believe Philip as he preached the good news about the kingdom of God and the name of Jesus Christ." In places where the Greek word *euangelizo* occurs, as in Luke 4:43, 8:1, 16:6 and so on, the verb is in the middle voice, which characteristically is used of a subject acting in some way that concerns itself or acting upon something that belongs to itself. Moulton describes middle voice simply as reflexive.[4] From several aspects, then, the combination of "preaching" and "bearing good news" carries a strong sense of Jesus proclaiming who he, himself, is. In Luke, he is the proclamation of good news.

The repeated use of *kai* to run clauses together is almost certainly a Semitism imitating Hebrew structure. As experts have noted, "a 'kai' before the finite verb represents a yet more literal translation of Hebrew idiom."[5] The running narrative creates a flowing motion from the preaching and bearing of good news to "the Twelve" and "some women." The result of these structures is the achievement of an effect the redactor seems to have had in mind in composing this section. The dramatis personae are placed clearly in the forefront and there is no way to mistake the fact that "the Twelve" and "some women" are equally recipients of the proclamation and the good news. They were chosen deliberately because the description portrays an itinerant preacher who had women in his entourage, contrary to rabbinic law and probably contrary to custom in the Roman Empire of the first century of the Christian era.

The women, then, are just as much part of Jesus' band of disciples as are "the Twelve." It is immensely interesting that the expression "Twelve" is used instead of "apostles," since these terms are often used interchangeably. The significance of "the Twelve" as sign of the new covenant built upon the tradition of twelve tribes of Israel was seen as central to God's plan for humankind. By placing the women side by side with "the Twelve" the redactor achieves the effect of including them in this new covenant and assigning them a role there similar to that assigned to "the Twelve." Along with some other points the Lukan author wished to make by means of this summary, is the fact that women were expected to minister as equal sharers of the new covenant, even supporting it through their own wealth.

In Luke 8:1–3, as always, the name of Mary of Magdala heads the list of women disciples of Jesus. It is noteworthy that her name precedes that of Joanna, the wife of Herod's steward, Chuza. It is certain that the wife of Herod's steward was a person of wealth and social, even political, standing. And the writer makes this very clear. For Mary of Magdala to have been listed before Joanna is another indication of Mary's standing. The inclusion of the names of Mary of Magdala and Susanna among those who supported Jesus and the disciples out of their own resources indicates that they, too, were women of wealth and, probably, of social standing. Mary could not have been of a higher social and economic standing than Herod's steward's wife because there were no places available that were higher than that. Mary is known to have come from a lowly area of Palestine, Galilee. Some other reality places her ahead of Joanna. Luke 8:1–3 tells us that Mary of Magdala was a person of greater importance in the early church than was Joanna, wife of Herod's steward.

The Lukan redactor, then, had several important reasons for including this summary that by vocabulary, style and content, can be seen to be "original Luke." It provides a generic description of Jesus' ministry of proclaiming the good news as an itinerant preacher who had a sizable number of disciples, both women and men.

It was necessary to give this description because it was contrary to the mores of the day. Mary of Magdala is given pride of place here as in all the other references to her even though Joanna surely out-ranked her socially, economically and politically. The narrative sequence of which these verses are a part seems to have the purpose of defining and describing the discipleship group. The passage fore-shadows and prepares for the crucifixion, burial and resurrection narratives, but one of its primary purposes seems to be to authenti-cate the presence of women disciples with Jesus during his Galilean ministry. This prepares for their presence at the final events.

Crucifixion and Burial Narrative

The Lukan narratives of the events at the death of Jesus and at the burial differ in some substantial ways from the same narratives in Mark and Matthew. The Lukan account stresses the role of wit-nesses in all three incidents where the women appear (Luke 23:49; 23:55–56; 24:10–11). In Luke's twenty-third chapter, there are several witnesses present at the death of Jesus. The centurion witnesses to the innocence of Jesus and thus participates in the effort to assign guilt for the execution of Jesus—the Jews who handed Jesus over are responsible for Jesus' death. This Roman can proclaim Jesus innocent. A group of spectacle hunters are deeply affected by the manner of Jesus' death, and return home "beating their breasts" (Luke 23:48). A group of acquaintances, *gnostoi,* observe the crucifixion. The acquaintances, it should be observed, are neither disciples nor followers. The Greek word *gnostoi* literally means "those who were known." The women are twice described by the much more significant word "followers," in Greek *akolouthein,* which, by the time of the gospel writings, had become a technical word for disciples (*akolouthein,* to walk behind or follow, was frequently used in the New Testament as a specialized term for following Jesus).[6] In verse 49 of chapter 23 the women are referred to as those who had followed (*"sunakolouthousai"*) him from Galilee, and again, in verse 55, the word *katakolouthesasai* is used almost redundantly. The women are said to have come with Jesus (*"suneleluthuiai"*), so the clause reads, "the women who were following after him came with him from Galilee."[7] The *akolouthein* compounds accentuate the specific aspect of discipleship that involves being with the master; "this verb (akolouthein) characterizes the central quality of existence as a disciple."[8] As the Lukan redactor describes the scene, the witnesses to the death of Jesus were male acquaintances and female disciples. The spectacle seekers were overcome and returned to their homes performing the traditional sign of repentance, beating their breasts. The women observed the placement of the body and went off to buy and prepare spices. The centurion proclaimed Jesus innocent. The reaction of the acquaintances is not described.

In the death-and-burial stories and at the beginning of the empty-tomb narrative, the role of Mary of Magdala melds into the group of devout women followers of Jesus. Nonetheless, the fact that she leads the list the first time they are mentioned and again in the empty-tomb pericope substantiates her place as leader of this group. She is key to understanding the role of a group of women followers who ministered to Jesus and his disciples in Galilee.

Galilee is significant in the Lukan narrative as it is in the other synoptics. It is so important that it probably constitutes a "genuine memory of an actual ministry."[9] Galilee is the place from which the ministry of Jesus stems and it is known to have been an area, part of which at least, survived the Jewish Wars or was able to rebuild after those wars. By the time of the writing of the Lukan gospel, it had become identified as the place where Jesus' ministry originated and was to continue: "Men of Galilee, why are you standing there looking at the sky?" (Acts 1:11). Magdala was a town in Galilee and the citizen by whose name it is remembered was foremost among those disciples. It remains to question if there were additional reasons why the writer felt it important to identify the women as those who had been with Jesus in Galilee. If, indeed, he is making a distinction between the acquaintances who manifest no special reaction and the women who had followed and witnessed the events, there may be a hint of the possible conflict between the church in Jerusalem and the church in Galilee that is sometimes discussed. The writer seems to be making a point that the women had been with Jesus in Galilee. The fact of their having traveled with Jesus was so completely countercultural that they may represent the Galilean church at the crucifixion scene. Mary of Magdala, women, Galilee, witnesses to death, burial and resurrection—Luke connects all of these narrative elements. He places all of Jesus' ministry prior to the journey to Jerusalem in Galilee with the one exception of the crossing of the lake to the territory of the Gerasenes (Luke 8:26–39). The women are consistently identified as having come from Galilee and the messenger at the empty tomb reminds them that Jesus had promised resurrection when they had all been in Galilee.

These references to Galilee may have several meanings:

1. Galilee was the place where Jesus and his followers met those with great needs.
2. Galilee was the historic locale of Jesus' public life.
3. "The women" were prominent in Galilee after 70 CE.
4. Galilee was rebuilt and flourished after 70 CE. Jerusalem was not and did not.
5. Resurrection faith was somehow connected with the Galilean ministry.

Any or all of these may be relevant as there can be no question but that the writer of the Lukan narrative took the prominence of Galilee very seriously. Resurrection was to be associated with Galilee and Mary of Magdala and the other women were connected with Galilee.

The Empty-Tomb Narrative

The Lukan empty-tomb narrative is markedly different from the accounts in Mark and Matthew, even though the basic framework of the story obviously came from the same tradition. The women are not named until after they have made the announcement to the "eleven and the others" (Luke 24:9). It is made clear that they intend to anoint the body of Jesus even though this purpose is not specifically stated. The role of the women is different here from that in Mark and Matthew. They come with spices but manifest no concern at all about rolling back the stone. They enter the tomb without hesitation or fear and become "perplexed," literally, "at a loss." This reaction is quite subdued compared to that of Mary of Magdala in the fourth gospel. It is clear that the stone has significance in all four accounts and in all of them it has been rolled back. Each redactor uses this detail to his own purpose: In Mark, it reflects the women's lack of understanding; in Matthew, it is connected with apocalyptic signs; in Luke, it seems relatively unimportant, and in the fourth gospel it provides the impetus to the story of two "beloved disciples."

In Luke's account, two men appear. Later in Luke 24:23 they will be called angels, whose appearance is such that the women bow their faces to the ground in a gesture that is a typical reaction to manifestations of divinity in the Hebrew scriptures (as in Genesis 18:2, Joshua 5:14; Judges 13:20 and so forth). The question these two men pose to the women is an extended refinement of the query posed in Mark and Matthew. They ask, "Why do you seek the living among the dead?"

The men insinuate that the women should have anticipated resurrection. The reason that they should have anticipated it follows immediately in the repetition of the Passion prediction as found earlier in Luke 9:22, "The Son of Man must suffer greatly and be rejected by the elders, the chief priests, and the scribes, and be killed and on the third day be raised." The prediction is repeated in Luke 17:25 and 18:32–33. Verse 8 of Luke's empty-tomb account records that the women did then remember these words. Obviously they had been active participants in these earlier scenes. "And returning from the tomb they told all this to the eleven and to all the rest." The statement is so totally unadorned, direct, unemotional, that it seems to be a necessity of the narrative, perhaps only that.

The message from the men/angels is not the same as in Mark and in Matthew. In those accounts the women are told not to be frightened, that the messengers know that they seek Jesus who was crucified and that he had risen as is proven by the empty tomb. The Lukan redactor has developed this message into a reflection on the mystery of resurrection and on the fulfillment of Passion predictions. The redactor of the fourth gospel stressed other elements such as the message of resurrection embodied in Jesus himself. The messengers had become redundant.

The Lukan stress on resurrection as the fulfillment of Jesus' predictions is unique. If the empty-tomb story is read in connection with the Emmaus story which follows it immediately (Luke 24:13–35), the redactional effort to portray Jesus as the fulfillment of his own predictions becomes pronounced. The development of this theme provides a narrative unity to the crucifixion, burial and empty-tomb account in Luke. It makes the contrast with the apostles' lack of belief more stark, even though they had heard the predictions just as the women had.

The women deliver the message "to the eleven and all the others" (Luke 24:9). The precision evident in the number, eleven, helps to make "all the others" seem a deliberate precision also. The others would seem to be a specific group of people, a gathering of disciples among whom were a sizable number of women who had followed from Galilee. Near the end of the empty-tomb pericope, the women are named by Luke in a structure different from that used by Mark and Matthew, who begin their narratives by listing the names of the women. One effect of listing them at the end is to unite the three stories—crucifixion, burial, empty tomb—around the story of the women. This stresses the role they play precisely as women. Despite variations in details, the role of Mary of Magdala, sometimes together with other women, is to recognize that Jesus had risen and to carry the message of resurrection to the other disciples.

The lack of an appearance sequence, or perhaps the development of it into the Emmaus story, is noteworthy. No appearance occurs at the scene of the empty tomb. The writer's interest seems to be elsewhere, in showing that Jesus had predicted the resurrection and that his disciples should have been prepared for it. The result of the message is disbelief. Peter's running to the tomb is detailed in this manner only in Luke. Peter runs to the tomb, sees the burial cloths, and goes home amazed. The story shares many elements with the twentieth chapter of the fourth gospel. Peter sees (the verb is *blepo* because a sense perception is involved). He sees the burial cloths but there is no indication of belief on Peter's part— he is simply amazed.

Luke's empty-tomb narrative, then, is different from the parallel narratives in Mark and Matthew in significant ways. Luke carefully describes the women as those who had ministered to and with Jesus when he was in Galilee. While Mary of Magdala maintains her place as the first named and in the same name-formula as in all the other accounts, she melds into the picture of the groups of women who are identified as disciple-followers of Jesus. They seem more deliberate about buying and preparing spices ahead of time than do the women in Mark and Matthew. They are not fearful of the empty tomb but only of the men in dazzling apparel. The message the women receive and relay is a remembrance of the predictions Jesus has made. The empty-tomb narrative in Luke, then, takes on something of the nature of a proof text rather than a statement of the reality of resurrection as it does in Mark and Matthew.

The Lukan message of the men/angels differs also from that given in Mark and Matthew. In the fourth gospel there is no response from the two angels because Mary's attention turns elsewhere. In Matthew and Mark the messengers admonish the women to cease being amazed and afraid and to recognize the reality that Jesus has risen. In Luke the message is quite different: the women are asked why they seek the living among the dead and are then reminded that Jesus had told them this mystery would occur. Mary of Magdala and the other women are called upon to remember what Jesus had been teaching. The members of the early church knew that the women had heard Jesus speak of his coming suffering and could have been expected to remember it.

Conclusions

The overall effect of the synoptic empty-tomb narratives is important. The Markan account ends with a restatement of the basic theme that human beings through their own power are not able to comprehend the meaning of Jesus Christ even when the signs before them are clear. The Matthean account introduces elements of the apocalyptic in order to direct attention to future appearances in Galilee. The Lukan writer is manifestly interested in the unbelief of the disciples and the fact that, having heard Jesus' own prediction of his suffering, they could have been expected to understand it. As will be demonstrated, in the fourth gospel the focus is on the beloved disciple, who sees and believes, and on Mary of Magdala, who changes herself almost instantaneously from a devoted follower trying to find the dead body to the primary messenger of resurrection. In all four accounts there is strong evidence of the place that Mary of Magdala held in the early church. She is the leader of the women, she is the first to know of resurrection and she is the primary bearer of resurrection witness to the "eleven."

Another interesting facet of these stories is the contrast created several times between the unbelief of the disciples, of Peter and of the "other disciple," and the belief of the women. The Markan author, for redactional purposes, leaves the women in a state of fear, but not necessarily of unbelief. The Matthean author leaves them, having enjoyed an appearance complete with embraces, to carry the good news to his brothers who later on are still doubting (Matt 28:17). The Lukan writer ends the empty-tomb narrative with the "apostles" accusing the women of carrying what the King James and other versions translate as an "idle tale" (Luke 24:11). The fourth gospel leaves the narrative with Mary having announced the resurrection as well as her own apostleship. The reaction of the disciples to whom she has been sent is not recorded. However, previously, both Peter and the "other disciple" have seen something and then have gone home. It is impossible to escape the conclusion that the early church understood the resurrection through the instrumentality of Mary of Magdala and possibly of some other women. None of the male apostles, disciples, "the Twelve," appear as believers in these narratives, nor as messengers of resurrection faith.

There are many possible reasons for the unbelief of apostles and disciples. Even Peter evinces only amazement, not belief, at the evidence around him. It is important to avoid a gender qualification for belief but that fact leads to the question, why were the women the witnesses and the bearers of the message to the disciples? If, indeed, Mary of Magdala was the historical primary messenger, and this study asserts that that is a viable assumption based upon the evidence, the reason is not gender but the early church's perception of where belief in the resurrection had its origin. It came through Mary of Magdala whose role is developed in several different manners.

The synoptic empty-tomb narratives have the following in common: the fact that Mary of Magdala was the first witness to the resurrection, the presence of the large stone which had to be removed, the presence of divine messengers, the mention of Galilee and the sending of the women to the disciples. They differ in some theological presuppositions: Mark stresses difficulty in understanding and disbelief among those who had most reason to understand; Matthew stresses the apocalyptic nature of the event and the promise of an appearance in Galilee; Luke directly employs the faithful feminine messengers as foils to the lack of faith of the apostles and the fact that Jesus had foretold his resurrection. Mary of Magdala is primary in all of these accounts.

CHAPTER 5

Mary of Magdala in the Fourth Gospel

It has already been noted that the role of Mary of Magdala in the empty-tomb narratives holds the key to the questions of her role in the early church, because her presence at the empty tomb is noted in all four canonical gospels and in the extant apocryphal gospels, and her name survived the processes of revision and redaction that took place for some time in the early church. In the process of revision, women's names were often lost, as for example, that of the Samaritan woman at the well (John 4); the widow of Naim (Luke 7); the woman who anointed Jesus' head at Bethany (Mark 14). But the name, Mary of Magdala, remained. Her presence cannot be ignored.[1]

There do not seem to be any clear avenues of approach to the reason or reasons why Mary of Magdala is primary witness to, and messenger of, the resurrection. This role is recorded of her in all the gospel accounts. Quite possibly the clearest avenue of approach is the obvious one, that indeed, Mary of Magdala was both primary witness to the mystery of resurrection and the primary bearer of this revelation to the disciples. Her primacy is maintained through the crucifixion, burial and empty-tomb narratives in all four gospels. In the synoptic gospels the three events flow together into one unified narrative. They do not do this in the fourth gospel.

Women are mentioned only at the crucifixion and at the empty tomb, and their presence in each case has its own purpose.

The realization that the fourth gospel is, as Brown has said, "startlingly different from the other gospels in its presentation of Jesus and startlingly different from the Pastoral Epistles and the Book of Acts in its view of ecclesiastical realities"[2] is so obvious as to be rarely challenged. Mary of Magdala also is portrayed differently in the fourth gospel.

There is no specific mention in the fourth gospel of the women who ministered to Jesus in Galilee, even though there are many women involved in the events pictured in this gospel. It is noteworthy that in this gospel major proclamations about Jesus' identity are made by women. Samaritan people begin to believe in Jesus through the testimony of the woman at the well: "Come and see a man who told me everything I have done. Could he possibly be the Messiah?" (John 4:29). Martha voices the confession assigned to Peter in the other gospels, "Yes, Lord, I have come to believe that you are the Messiah, the Son of God, the one who is coming into the world" (John 11:27). Mary of Magdala makes the solemn proclamation of resurrection, "I have seen the Lord" (John 20:18).

Crucifixion Narrative

In the fourth gospel, there is only one mention of Mary of Magdala prior to the empty-tomb narrative. This occurs at the crucifixion scene (John 19:25): "Standing by the cross of Jesus were his mother and his mother's sister, Mary the wife of Clopas, and Mary of Magdala." There have been lengthy scholarly discussions of whether this is to be read as two, three or four women. It is not necessary to discuss that question here because it is clear that Mary of Magdala was one woman present at the crucifixion scene as was Mary, the mother of Jesus.

The structure of the crucifixion scene in the fourth gospel is instructive. The actual crucifixion is reported in a subordinate clause because the focus is on the casting of lots for Jesus' garment as this action reflects Psalm 22. "When the soldiers had crucified Jesus, they took his clothes and divided them into four shares..." (John 19:23). Then, in what must be regarded as a late addition to the text, the scene between Jesus and his mother with the beloved disciple is recounted. Verses 25–27 of chapter 19 are clearly a separate entity intended to depict the gift of Jesus' mother to the beloved disciple. It is to be noted that neither Jesus' mother nor the beloved disciple is referred to by name in this gospel. As was demonstrated above, the lack of name for Jesus' mother must be seen against the consistent use of the topographical form to identify Mary of Magdala.[3] After the break for the story of Jesus and his mother, the fourth gospel returns to the narrative of the actual crucifixion. The role of Mary of Magdala must be seen in light of this unique description of the mother of Jesus.

The event has significance in terms of the role of Mary of Magdala. The practice of listing names is the same here as in the synoptic gospels, the dramatis personae are simply named. No explanation is given nor is an introduction. The mother of Jesus had not appeared in this gospel since the wedding at Cana recorded in the second chapter. Evidently these women were well enough known to the Johannine community that explanations were superfluous. Their identity and the question of whether there were two, three or four of them, are modern problems. Those who formulated this gospel evidently knew these women and understood the construction of the scene.

The writer of the fourth gospel tells us that the women were "standing by the cross" (John 19:25). In Greek, the preposition *para* with a dative is translated "near"—not with a spatial meaning, but referring to the relationship of persons.[4] Since it is quite unlikely that the executioners would allow women, or any onlookers, to stand in the immediate vicinity of the cross, the meaning becomes even clearer that this is a personal, intimate, close interaction between Jesus and those whom he loved. There is no mention of the presence of the beloved disciple until Jesus addresses him. This contributes to keeping the focus of the dialogue on Jesus and his mother. So, the use of the preposition *para,* and the presence of the beloved disciple with Jesus and Mary of Magdala, paints a picture of Jesus with "his own"—a picture bearing a resemblance to the portrayal at the wedding feast at Cana. Established here is an undercurrent of close, personal relationship also found in the encounter between the risen Lord and Mary of Magdala in chapter 20.

The purpose of verse 25 is to establish the presence of Jesus' mother so that the gift to the beloved disciple can be made. That fact might make it even more significant that other women are included in the list. If the only concern of the event is the gift of Jesus' mother to the beloved disciple, why are the other women present? Certainly one would expect a companion to a woman who is watching the execution of her son, and her sister would be the most likely candidate to be with her. The fact that she or possibly another woman, Mary, the wife of Clopas, needed no other introduction indicates that she was a person of some prominence and her presence at the crucifixion would not seem inappropriate. But why is Mary of Magdala present? She is not a relative, nor is there any evidence given that she would be a support to the grieving mother. Again, the lack of any explanation of her presence indicates that it was not surprising. There are several possible explanations for the inclusion of Mary of Magdala in this scene. One is that she was so important in the early church that it was a sign of her position and of the respect due to her that she be included in such a dramatic scene. Another possible explanation is that she was so important at the time of Jesus that her presence would be taken for granted. And probably there was a historical recollection that Mary had been present at the actual crucifixion. Each of these reasons would indicate how very important Mary of Magdala was, either in Jesus' own time, or at the time of the writing of the gospels. In all probability, all three explanations are operative here.

The presence of women standing near the cross of Jesus is important to the theology and understandings of the community from which this gospel derives. The questions to be raised are not about historicity but about how this community saw the relationships between Jesus and his own, between Jesus and those whom he loved. The Johannine author uses the term "disciple" inclusively. He never uses the term "apostle." In the center of the final scene of Jesus' pre-resurrection earthly life stands his mother, who this community evidently saw as important to Jesus' human relationships; the unknown Mary who is her sister; the beloved disciple, and Mary of Magdala. They personify the relationship of Jesus with those, "who did accept him," and to whom "he gave power to become children of God" (John 1:12). Margaret Davies sums it up well:

> Their presence as witnesses, in the absence of the disciples, serves to guarantee that Jesus died and was buried, and that it was his tomb that was empty.[5]

The Empty-Tomb Narrative

It is generally accepted today that the empty-tomb narrative of the fourth gospel contains a pre-redactional story or group of stories that come from the earliest strata of the tradition. Scholars have long been involved in a process of identifying pre-redactional stories, seams, separate pericope and relationships of the synoptic gospels to the fourth gospel accounts.[6] Some of this scholarship is germane to the question of the role of Mary of Magdala.

There is a wide variety of opinion about the nature of the empty-tomb narrative related in John 20:1–18. Opinions range from belief that the fourth gospel's account is the earliest to the view that it is the latest version and the one most modified by redactors. Others believe that it is composed of a variety of segments from both early and late traditions, or that it is the result of traditional material used by each of the evangelists who reworked it according to specific theological outlooks. Frans Neirynck has proposed that there is a direct connection between the fourth gospel account of the empty-tomb story and the synoptic accounts.[7]

Questions of sources and comparative order of texts often yield murky results. However, there seems to be sufficient evidence to assert that the account of the events at the empty tomb in the fourth gospel is early and that it contains elements in common with the synoptic accounts. Possibly pre-redactional stories underlie all four of the gospel accounts. So, while the fourth gospel seems to have portions that came from an independent source, it also has much in common with the synoptic gospels. The important point here is that the empty-tomb narrative in the fourth gospel comes from an early pre-redactional source or at least shares passages with some such source. It contains early traditions. So, rather than thinking that the fourth gospel account melded two or three women disciples into one who went out early to the tomb, it is possible to reflect that the account of Mary of Magdala's encounter with the risen Christ is the original story and that the synoptic gospels expanded the number of women participants in their accounts.

While opinions about sources and chronological order vary widely, opinions about the structure of John 20:1–18, the empty-tomb narrative, vary much less significantly. Almost without question, scholars agree that the story found in verses 3–10, the race of Peter and the "other disciple," is an addition to the original pre-redactional empty-tomb narrative.[8] Equally respected is the contention that the encounter of Mary of Magdala with Jesus in verses 14–18 is a separate appearance story, albeit one highly atypical because, as C. H. Dodd has written, "the narrator has succeeded in conveying not so much incidents as psychological traits."[9]

Verses 1 and 2 of chapter 20 form an introduction to both stories, that of the race of the two disciples and that of the appearance to Mary of Magdala. It cannot be assumed that verse 1 provides an introduction to the appearance narrative in verses 11 to 18 and that verse 2 forms an introduction to the pericope found in verses 3 to 10. It is impossible to consider these verses separated from each other without changing them extensively. The most obvious reason is that verse 2, "so she ran and went to Simon Peter and to the other disciple whom Jesus loved" (John 20:2) does not make sense without the description in verse 1 of Mary's journey to the tomb and her finding the stone rolled back. The substrata of elements that can be discerned here may be relevant to a study of the process by which this chapter was formed, but they are not considered here because the focus here is solely on understanding the role of Mary of Magdala.

In the final redaction of the fourth gospel, verses 1 and 2 of chapter 20 form an introduction to the whole narrative passage. Verses 11–13 form an "angelophany" and are a vestigial remnant of a traditional story that was too strong in the tradition to be omitted but in this case fails to advance the narrative. The structure of John 20:1–18, then, has four parts. Verses 1 and 2 form the introduction to the whole; the stories of the race of the two disciples to the tomb and the appearance to Mary of Magdala form two separate-but-related appearance narratives, and verses 11 to 13 form the seam between these two important stories. It is apparent that there exists some kind of parallel, or at least significant, relationship between the two main stories.

Verses 1 and 2 and verses 11 to 13 are employed to bring unity and coherence to the two separate pericopes that the redactor has chosen to put together in this structure for his own purpose. The first verse of chapter 20 is almost completely at one with the opening verses of the synoptic gospels in specifying time. In Mark and Matthew the emphasis is on the fact that the Sabbath was over; in Luke and John, it is simply "the first day of the week." The redactor of the fourth gospel includes the comment that "it was still dark." The theme of darkness and light in the fourth gospel is so pronounced that this clearly contributes to the contrast between the darkness of the entombment and the light of resurrection. In John 1:5, "the light shines in the darkness, and the darkness has not overcome it;" in John 6:17, "it had already grown dark and Jesus had not yet come to them;" in John 8:12, "whoever follows me will not walk in darkness;" in John 12:35, "whoever walks in the dark does not know where he is going" and in John 12:46, "I came into the world as light, so that everyone who believes in me might not remain in darkness." The dramatic impact of the reference to darkness at the empty tomb adds a new dimension to the time frame without changing the essential time element of the synoptic accounts. Mary of Magdala approaches the empty tomb in darkness. It is clear that no woman would venture out into the darkness in the time of Jesus or in the postapostolic time when this account may have been written. Thus, the purpose is clearly to indicate something of Mary's frame of mind.

The problem of the stone covering the entrance to the tomb is mentioned in all of the gospel accounts. In Mark's account the women are mistakenly concerned with the problem of finding someone to roll the stone away for them. It has already been rolled away. In Matthew's account the women observe the rolling away of the stone amid apocalyptic signs of strength and power. In Luke there does not seem to have been any concern about rolling the stone away nor surprise that it had been removed. In the fourth gospel the fact of the stone's having been "removed from the tomb"

(John 20:1), provides the impetus to the entire sequence of events. Mary jumps to the conclusion that someone had stolen the body from the tomb. This becomes a major theme in the fourth gospel account of the events at the empty tomb. Mary repeatedly concentrates on the fact that the body had been stolen. This redactor is determined to show that Mary of Magdala is exclusively concerned with recovering the body of Jesus. The emphasis starts in the introductory verses.

Without any further investigation, Mary runs to Simon Peter and the "other disciple" whose presence in this scene is clearly redactional, "So she ran and went to Simon Peter and to the other disciple whom Jesus loved" (John 20:2). This is the only place in the gospels where a male disciple, other than Peter, actually comes to the tomb. In Luke's account Peter goes alone to the tomb after Mary of Magdala and the other women bring news of the resurrection to the assembled disciples. In Mark the women are told to carry the message to "his disciples and Peter," but they do not do it. In Matthew they are sent to "his disciples" (Matt 28:7) and later "to my brothers" (Matt 28:10). In Luke they are not sent but they return "to the eleven and to all the others" (Luke 24:9). In none of these passages is another disciple mentioned; the reference to him is unique to the fourth gospel and is part of the presentation of this unidentified disciple in the fourth gospel. It is possible that he is inserted into this gospel because of the race theme that permeates (John 20:3–10), or that the presence of this other disciple provides the reason for the race theme. It may also indicate a type of tension between those early Christians who looked to Peter's legacy and those who looked to that of some other disciple.

The pronoun "we" in verse 2 is puzzling, "They have taken the Lord from the tomb and we do not know where they put him" (John 20:2). Only Mary has been mentioned in the opening verses and so the pronoun seems inaccurate. The tradition underlying the synoptic accounts may have contained a list of two or three women who accompanied Mary but the writer of the twentieth chapter of the fourth gospel wants to have Mary alone for the encounter with Jesus. The most satisfactory explanation, then, for the use of the plural pronoun is that "I" and "we" can be used interchangeably in Aramaic.[10] The writer's emphasis is on the fact that Mary of Magdala had only one thought in mind, that is to find the dead body of Jesus. This was her only concern. Since this account is probably the earliest of the empty-tomb narratives, or at least is based upon the earliest accounts, the fact that Mary of Magdala goes alone to the empty tomb looking for the dead body of Jesus may well be the original tradition.

The two main pericopes—the race to the tomb in verses 3 to 10 and the encounter between Jesus and Mary of Magdala in verses 14 to 18—are both complementary and contrasting. They are of comparable length; they both utilize the Johannine device of one on one; they are both concerned with seeing and believing; a beloved disciple is the chief participant in each. These basic similarities make the contrasts more meaningful.

The Race Narrative

The "race narrative" begins in verse 3: "So Peter and the other disciple went out and came to the tomb." Mary of Magdala is removed from the scene by the simple device of failing to mention her and she takes no part in the action after she has delivered the message. The two disciples are not only center stage but they quickly assume something of a competitive stance.

In the Nestle-Aland text[11] there are 113 words in this pericope. Twenty of those words are nouns. Peter and the "other disciple" are referred to by seven of the nouns, all of the rest refer to things: "tomb" occurs four times; "linen cloths" three times; "napkin," "head," "place," "scripture" and "the dead" occur once each. The consistency of references to things produces a somewhat ambiguous tone. Urgency, haste, even competition are evident but all third-person references depict static things that reflect the writer's concern with the empty tomb and the missing body. Mary had set the pattern for this in the opening scene by her hasty conclusion that the body had been stolen, based solely on the fact that the stone had been rolled away from the entrance to the tomb. While the two disciples act with urgency and haste, the third-person references are all to the accoutrements of death. They are all concrete and static, objective and impersonal.

The atmosphere of urgency and haste that contrasts with the static third-person references is created mostly by the use of action verbs. Nine times one of the forms of the Greek verb *erxomai* is used to describe the going and coming of the two disciples. The verb for *run* is used twice. The only other finite verbs are "he saw" in verse 3, and "had been" in verse 7. The verb which occurs in verse 8c occurs also in the final verse of the segment when Mary of Magdala declares to the disciples, "I have seen the Lord" (John 20:18). When Peter and the "other disciple" saw the burial cloth, the Greek word *blepo* was used. When *blepo* is used it involves sense perception. Peter saw (*theorai*) burial cloths as had the "other disciple" before him. The verbs are in the historical present, a customary usage in the fourth gospel.

Verse 8c is different from the rest of this pericope for several reasons. Verse 8c, "he saw and believed," differs because the verb "to see" is *horao*, used without an object. The aorist tense is used for both verbs and the narrator-observer slips into omniscient observer for the only time in the pericope. The two verbs "saw" and "believed" are without direct objects and thus throw open a wide area of possible meaning as well as a wide area for ambiguity. These differences between verse 8c and the rest of the pericope provide sufficient evidence to suggest a redactional addition to an original narrative.

"He saw" in verse 8c translates the Greek verb *horao,* which is employed when a sensory perception is not necessarily involved in the action of seeing. The redactor avoids a direct object after "he saw," and he also avoids it after "he believed." It is, therefore, indefinite what the disciple saw and what he believed. Ambiguity grows. The voice heard in this entire story has been carefully limited to the role of narrator-observer. Facts are related without editorial comment and without any effort to explore the workings of the disciples' minds. Verse 8c shifts notably away from this basic point of view as the disciple is described as one who believed. Verse 8c achieves precision and emphasis from simplicity of structure, from the choice of verbs and from the use of the simple past tense form, the aorist.

The differences in verb usage, in the choice of verbs, and the use of the omniscient narrator combine to raise some question about the relationship between verse 8c and the rest of the account. Whether or not it is an insertion, there is sufficient evidence to indicate that it differs from the surrounding narrative. Possibly this shows that, at some level of composition, an effort was made to designate the unnamed disciple whom Jesus loved as the first to believe in resurrection—notwithstanding the difficulty produced by the seeming contradiction between "he saw and believed" (John 20:8c), and "they did not yet understand the scripture that he had to rise from the dead" (John 20:9).

Verse 9 is an editorial comment that seems to excuse the two disciples from guilt for their lack of understanding. This is jarring because it follows immediately upon the statement that the unnamed disciple "saw and believed" adding to the ambiguity of the passage. The final words of verse 9 assert that Jesus "had to rise" (*dei anastanai*). This adds a sense of necessity for the resurrection that is not discernible elsewhere in the passage.

In the "race narrative" a lack of secondary descriptive details suggests a single purpose in the mind of the author. The race of the two disciples and the fact that the "other disciple" saw and believed was the author's primary emphasis. Raymond Brown saw a possible connection due to the love the "other disciple" experienced "which outran the love Peter knew."[12] However, the economy of detail and expression leaves many unanswered questions. For example, we are not told where Mary located the disciples, if there were other disciples present and, if so, why they did not come to the tomb. We are not told where Peter and the "other disciple" went after their visit. We are not told their response to what they had experienced. We can only guess why the beloved disciple could outrun Peter and we know nothing of Peter's reaction to what he saw in the tomb. We aren't even told what the "other disciple" saw or what he believed.

The reading of this account, with close attention to the literary characteristics and to the things that are not said, leads to the conclusion that the story was placed in this narrative sequence for reasons other than the attempt to explain the resurrection or to explain its effects upon the disciples. The major emphasis seems to have been on the race and its results, the seeing and believing by the "other disciple." The possibility that some kind of competition existed between the two disciples is at least possible—if not during the actual resurrection scene, then during the time of developing perspectives in the early communities. Perhaps there was also concern to present the primacy of love since the "other disciple" is the one "whom Jesus loved." If, indeed, this account is paralleled by the encounter story of Mary of Magdala and Jesus, there is perhaps a hint of a parallel between a male beloved disciple and a female beloved disciple.

Here, as elsewhere in the fourth gospel, the beloved disciple is carefully not named. His waiting for Peter to enter the tomb first is not explained in any way. If it is an act of deference, this is not made clear in the text. The other possibility, of course, is that some type of competition existed among the followers of Peter and those who followed the "beloved disciple." This type of competition was not unknown in the early church as we read in First Corinthians and as we find in the apocryphal gospels. This fact might well shed some light on the exact role played by Mary of Magdala in the early church. If such a polemic lies in the background of this community's presentation of the empty-tomb narrative, a nice balance may be said to have been achieved by the device of having the "other disciple" the first to arrive at the tomb; Peter is the first to enter and inspect the entire scene, but the "other disciple" is the one to see and believe. If there were competition between the two sets of disciples, and if that reflected a situation at the time of the writing of the final redaction, then it becomes possible to suspect that the paralleling of the race account with the appearance to Mary of Magdala has some similar background.

Verse 10 is a closure. "Then the disciples returned home." It is strange because so little has been revealed of the responses of the two disciples and even of the causes of those responses. Very directly the verse provides an objective statement of withdrawal from the scene by the two who have been the center of the action since verse 3. Verse 10 is so complete a closure, and the story is so self-contained, that the whole story could be excised from the text without any immediate loss of continuity or of meaning in terms of resurrection. Says John Alsup: "In short, the 'race story' affords a later broadening to the spectrum of witness to the empty tomb by adding redactional, secondary support to apostolic authority."[13]

The Appearance to Mary

Important parallels and contrasts exist between this hybrid empty-tomb narrative and the appearance-encounter of Jesus with Mary of Magdala that constitutes the second main element of the fourth gospel's use of the empty-tomb tradition. In the Nestle-Aland text, verses 14 to 18 of chapter 20 contain 108 words, comparable in length to the race story's 113 words. In a manner similar to the handling of the race story, the appearance-encounter story engages two persons in the action, and fits the pattern of seeing and believing. It also tells of an appearance to a "beloved disciple."

The appearance of Jesus to Mary of Magdala in verses 14 to 18 contains 21 nouns, one more than the number used in the race narrative. Here, however, all of the nouns save one refer to persons: Jesus is named five times; the Father occurs three times; Mary, God and Lord occur twice each; woman, gardener, Rabboni, teacher, brothers, disciples occur once each. The only exception to the use of these people-oriented nouns is the word, "Hebrew," which is found in an editorial comment in verse 16. The race story with all its urgency and haste is oriented toward the accoutrements of death and burial while the appearance story is totally oriented toward people.

Verbs are more prominent in the appearance story than in the race narrative. There are 25 finite verbs in verses 14 to 18 compared with 13 in verses 3 to 10. Forms of the verb "say" (*lego*) are used nine times, since the passage rests heavily upon a dramatic exchange of dialog. *Erxomai,* so prominent in the race story, occurs only once in the appearance story as Mary comes to the disciples and even, in this one instance, her journey is completely subordinate to her message. The verbs for "seeing" are used here as they are in the race narrative. When Mary enjoys a sense perception, when she sees someone she thinks is the gardener, the verb *theorei* is used, but when she announces the resurrection to Jesus' brothers, the verb used is a form of *horao* (*heoraka*). The two uses of the verb for "turning" carry a very significant burden of meaning.

One of the effects of the choice of nouns and verbs is to place this story in direct contrast with the race story. The urgency and haste of the two disciples, their coming and going, is without result: what they saw and what they believed is not recorded. The result of Jesus' appearance to Mary of Magdala is the announcement of the message of resurrection. The race narrative ends with the disciples going home. It reveals nothing of an end result—neither of their running nor of their relationship with the other disciples. The story of the appearance to Mary of Magdala, with its action almost totally encompassed by verbs of speaking, being, turning and seeing, bears very important results. Mary goes and proclaims the mystery of resurrection to the disciples.

Verses 14 to 18 describe personal encounter. In verse 14, Mary is "turned around." The verb is passive with a reflexive sense.[14] Literally, it reads, "Mary turned herself around." At this point she begins a movement away from her compulsion to find the body of Jesus, but she still attempts to obtain information from the person she believes to be the gardener. From this point on, the encounter becomes a fully personal reality. Everything focuses on the two people involved, Jesus and Mary of Magdala, and ends with Mary's mission to other people, the disciples. The entire incident is dramatic—Mary is in dialog with the supposed gardener and with Jesus when he has revealed himself to her. It is dynamic by the very quality of the verbal exchange. It is unified and conclusive: there are no leftover unanswered questions about primary matters. The narrative is clear, direct and of single purpose. The highly dramatic and intense final verse, when Mary announces the resurrection to the disciples, contrasts markedly with the bland "then the disciples returned home" (John 20:10).

After the race, Mary of Magdala is returned to the center of the action and she immediately enters into dialog, first with "two angels in white" (John 20:12), then with the person she assumes to be the gardener, and then with the risen Jesus whom she finally recognizes. It has already been noted that verses 11 to 13 constitute a seam, albeit one composed entirely of traditional materials. Verses 11 to 13 are important literarily because they refocus attention on Mary of Magdala and provide the setting for the encounter between Mary and the risen Jesus. Almost incidentally, they provide the place for the traditional presence of heavenly messengers.

Mary reappears in verse 11 just as suddenly as she had disappeared in verse 3. The two disciples are removed and they do not reappear. Mary stood outside the tomb—the verb for "stood" is pluperfect with the imperfect sense of a continued action in past time, "Mary was standing."[15] She was weeping. When she stooped to look into the tomb, as the "other disciple" had done, she saw (*theorei*) two angels. These angels are part of a biblical pattern of heavenly messengers who appear at revelatory moments in some type of dazzling attire. The exchange between Mary and the two angels who seem to speak in chorus, reinforces the motif of concern to locate the body of Jesus which had been taken from the tomb. The redactors are clearly concerned with this function of the empty-tomb narrative. The tomb was empty and Mary made strenuous and intense efforts to find the dead body. She did not succeed. The encounter with the heavenly messengers seems to lead nowhere in terms of Mary's quest. It provides another occasion for Mary to repeat her concern over the missing body. It also fulfills the demand of tradition in which the angelophany had a recognized place.

Some aspects of the personality of Mary of Magdala can be discerned from the narrative to this point. She is portrayed as a woman who feels intensely and who matches the intensity of her feeling with action—she searches persistently for Jesus' body. She remains at the tomb in contrast to the two disciples who return home almost immediately. She is not overawed by the presence of heavenly messengers and she does not allow them to distract her from her quest.

The actual appearance of Jesus to Mary of Magdala begins with the words, "When she had said this" (John 20:14). She then turns herself around, she turns from the tomb and from the messengers who have given her no assistance. She turns away from the place where they had laid him, from the tomb that has now served its purpose. The Greek verb used to describe Mary's turning from the tomb, *strepho,* often carries the meaning of changing one's manner or concern. Mary is reaching a critical point but she is still seeing, *theorei,* in the same way that Peter and the "other disciple" had seen the burial cloths lying. *Theoreo* describes sense perception and Mary's sense perception tells her that this is the gardener. Mary sees, (*theorei*) but she does not see (*horao*).

The lack of immediate recognition of the risen Lord is a recurring theme in many of the resurrection narratives. The two disciples walking to Emmaus do not know that Jesus is walking with them (Luke 24:13–35). Luke also tells us that the disciples did not believe the women's story of the empty tomb and that Peter, having gone to the tomb, reacts with amazement, not with belief. In the twenty-first chapter of the fourth gospel, the breakfast on the seashore scene, the disciples fail to recognize Jesus standing on the shore. Thus, Mary's failure to recognize Jesus fits a pattern that has a strongly theological intent. Scholars suggest that the Lord's body had been transformed. The point is emphasized by repeated failures to recognize him.[16]

Whatever else lies behind the narrative of the empty tomb, it is clear that the description of Mary of Magdala given there is what the early church wanted, even felt obliged to maintain. Mary is someone who feels intensely but does not panic; she is persistent but always courteous; she continues to search but without causing difficulty; she hopes to find the body of Jesus and will not relinquish this quest. Until the end, she is not expecting resurrection. "The tears, the grief, and the concern about Jesus' body are outstanding marks of Mary's experience."[17]

In John 20, verse 15 records a clear, direct address by Jesus to Mary of Magdala. He calls her "woman," as he had called his mother on two occasions—at the wedding feast in Cana described in John 2:4 ("Woman, how does your concern affect me?") and from the cross in John 16:26 ("Woman, behold your son"). In chapter 20 Jesus repeats the question asked by the angels in their very words: "Woman, why are you weeping?" (John 20:15). In both instances the address, "Woman," carries connotations of dignity and respect. Jesus addresses Mary of Magdala with the same dignity and respect with which he had addressed his mother.

Mary supposes the speaker to be the gardener. The redactor has prepared for this reference by mentioning the garden to which Jesus and the disciples went: "Jesus went out with his disciples across the Kidron valley to where there was a garden" (John 18:1), and by placing the narrative of the burial in a garden: "Now in the place where he had been crucified there was a garden..." (John 19:41). Since the whole empty-tomb narrative occurs in the garden, Mary's mistake can be taken to be quite natural. Two things are germane here. Mary is still not expecting to see Jesus, and she is not able to recognize the resurrected Lord simply by seeing (*theoreo*) him.

Mary's failure to recognize Jesus by the simple act of seeing him raises several important issues when played against the seeing and believing of the "other disciple" and the message of resurrection that is so often connected with seeing or appearing. Mary is so far from recognizing Jesus that she reiterates her plea for knowledge of the whereabouts of Jesus' body so that she may take it away. Even though she does not recognize Jesus, Mary addresses the gardener in a courteous term, "Sir" (*Kurie*). She is distressed but not panicky. She is persistent and will continue her search until some resolution is reached. She is not expecting any kind of miracle and she is not fearful as the absent disciples are. The structure of this appearance scene is meaningful. The narrative is simple and direct and the action of the incident is found in the dialog:

"Jesus said to her..."
"...turning herself she said to him..."
"Jesus said to her..."
"Mary of Magdala went and said to the disciples..."

These are clear, simple and direct statements. There are no interruptions, no modifiers, no intensifiers, no secondary details. This is wholly and simply encounter in dialog. Jesus calls Mary by name and she turns herself and completely changes her course of action. She had already made the physical move necessary to turn her attention away from the empty tomb and toward the person. The verb *strepho* carries the added connotation that she had changed her course of action. The reflexive quality of that verb imputes responsibility for the change to Mary herself. She turns herself and allows herself to be changed by a new, totally surprising reality. Now there is a new dimension to Mary of Magdala. She is able to turn to a new reality, one of which she has had no previous indication, that changes her entire life and engulfs her. The redactor has taken pains to prove that Mary did not expect resurrection. At this point, he pictures that she will change that expectation.

Raymond Brown points out that the title Mary gives to Jesus, "Rabbouni" is modest, "a title that is characteristic of the beginning of faith rather than of its culmination."[18] The word *Rabbouni* is Aramaic and is certainly meant to be a term of some intensity, even of endearment, "my teacher." Of course, some of the force of the endearment is mitigated by the scribal insertion, "which means Teacher" (John 20:16). However, the form of the word is familiar and expresses a personal relationship. It is a statement of personal encounter: Mary knows Jesus when he calls her by name. She employs a possessive form when responding to him.

Again simply and directly, Jesus responds to Mary in the troubling words, "Stop holding on to me" which reads more literally, "Do not keep clinging to me" (John 20:17). There have been many suggestions about the meaning of this imperative but underlying all the suggested meanings is the supposition that Mary had not yet understood the full import of what was occurring and that she had missed the transformation by which this resurrected Christ differed from the Jesus who had inhabited her world. It is an emphatic command: the implications are broad. The verb "do not keep clinging to me" is in the imperfect tense denoting a past action continuing into the present. Mary does not recognize Jesus by sight, so the present encounter does not match the encounters she had had with Jesus during his historical existence. But he has "not yet ascended to the Father," so his presence to Mary is neither totally human nor totally that of the risen Christ. She may not cling to the human Jesus and she may not yet cling to the risen and ascended Christ.

A sense of timelessness is created by the qualities of the verbs in verse 17, "Jesus said to her, 'Stop holding on to me, for I have not yet ascended to the Father. But go to my brothers and tell them, 'I am going to my Father and your Father, to my God and your God'" (John 20:17). Precision in regard to time is minimized by the use of the imperfect tense in "do not hold me" (*me mou haptou*). The imperfect tense denotes an action that continues, "a past action represented as being in progress."[19] The verb for "ascended" in verse 17 is in the perfect tense, "the perfect tense...denotes the continuance of completed action."[20] The other verbs in this verse—"go," and "tell them"—are in the imperfect tense; thus, all of the actions are progressive, they continue. To "go" and "tell them" are to be ongoing realities. The "them" refers to "my brothers," not to the apostles as in Luke 24:10 nor to the disciples and Peter as in Mark 16:7. Mary is to deliver the timeless message to his brothers, the *adelphous*. Moulton defines the word *adelphous* as "a brother; near kinsman or relative; one of the same nation or nature; one of equal rank and dignity; an associate, a member of a Christian community."[21] The message delivered to the brethren is an ongoing reality. Past actions that continue into the present, present action that has a strong future orientation, a precise description of a present event, all contribute to the sense of timelessness. Mary of Magdala is to carry the message that Jesus is ascending into a relationship, past as well as present and future, characterized by human elements as well as divine. The place to which Jesus is ascending is a person, his Father and Mary's Father and the Father of his brethren. Raymond Brown explains the timelessness and the personal relationship thus:

> When the risen Jesus has to explain to Magdalene that he is about to ascend, the emphasis is on the identification of the resurrection and the ascension, not the accidental time lag. In Johannine thought, there is only one risen Jesus, and he appears in glory in all his appearances.[22]

The message, so bound up with past, present and future time, is the quintessential message of resurrection-ascension. Jesus who lived among disciples such as Mary of Magdala, who died and was buried, has conquered time as well as death and is now present to his Father and to all of humanity. It is the role of Mary of Magdala to carry this message to the brethren and, hence, to all. The role of

Peter and the "other disciple" as portrayed in the fourth gospel, pales into insignificance beside this message and this messenger.

Verse 18 of chapter 20 closes the empty-tomb narrative of the fourth gospel. Literally, it reads, "Mary comes announcing to the disciples, 'I have seen the Lord.'" The participle used here for announcing (*angellousa*) is a form of the verb used for solemn proclamations. It occurs in Matt 28:11: "some of the guards went into the city and told (*apangeilan*) the chief priests all that had happened." It also occurs in the Markan appendix; when Mary of Magdala went and proclaimed the resurrection to the companions of Jesus, "she went and told (*apangeilen*) his companions" (Mark 16:10). Each time it bears the weight of a solemn proclamation and is used in these three narratives specifically in relation to the mystery of resurrection. Mary of Magdala is the dignified and solemn announcer of the mystery of resurrection.

The message that Mary carries to the disciples is of the clear and simple form that characterizes all of this pericope. Her words cannot be misinterpreted: they cannot be minimized. They are a direct proclamation of the fact that Mary has seen the Lord. The verb "seen" (*horao*) is the same verb used of the "other disciple" in verse 8c of John 20. It carries the sense of effective seeing.[23] Used in the perfect form in this passage, it connotes an effect upon the subject that Mary is proclaiming, that is, the total change in her life which has resulted from her encounter with the Lord through the startling reality of resurrection. It is obvious that she has been changed by the encounter. She is no longer distressed by the absence of Jesus; she is no longer searching for the dead body, and certainly she is not weeping. She is making a direct statement that she has seen the Lord. And that statement is critically important to defining her role in the early church and to answering questions about how her name remained in all of the empty-tomb narratives.

Conclusions

In First Corinthians 9:1, Paul asks, "Am I not free? Am I not an apostle? Have I not seen Jesus our Lord?" Through that series of questions, Paul is validating his own apostleship by the fact that he has seen the Lord. Is not Mary's apostleship also so validated? Fuller has written: "Apostles cannot come to faith as a result of the testimony of third parties. They must see and believe for themselves in order that they can provide first-hand witness."[24] Mary has seen for herself and she carries the message, she bears the witness. She fulfills the role of apostle by what she does as well as by what she has seen.

Some questions of historicity arise. The effort is not to attempt to establish historical fact in the background of the empty-tomb narrative, although that seems the most logical explanation of Mary's important presence. The effort is to show that, in the post–70 CE years when gospels were being written and redacted, the role of Mary of Magdala was known to be important and was so deeply embedded in the tradition that it could neither be omitted nor modified. Mary of Magdala was key to the realization of resurrection and thus, key witness in the empty-tomb narrative.

There is also the question of the quality of "firsthand"-type narrative sometimes attributed to the story of the appearance to Mary of Magdala. In a highly respected essay, "The Appearances of the Risen Christ: An Essay in Form-Criticism of the Gospels," C. H. Dodd wrote:

> Yet I confess that I cannot rid myself of the feeling (it can be no more than a feeling) that this pericope (John 20:11–17) has something indefinably first-hand about it. It stands, in any case, alone. There is nothing quite like it in the gospels.[25]

Even by reason of Dodd's own disclaimer, "it can be no more than a feeling," it is necessary to read his statement cautiously. However, it encourages consideration of the appearance to Mary of Magdala as either an eyewitness account or an account so strong in the oral tradition that it could not be omitted from the text. The use of present tense, extreme precision and economy of detail add to the eyewitness quality. It may even be that this pericope depicts a feminine beloved disciple whose experience parallels that of the "other disciple whom Jesus loved."

There are other indications that this may well be an eyewitness presentation. All other elements of story or description are eliminated from the account of the encounter between Jesus and Mary of Magdala. All other persons have been eliminated from the scene. Mary is pictured as someone who, almost desperately, pursues a single objective, finding the body of Jesus. The "brothers" are locked in a room as the redactor goes on to describe. In Luke's narrative, two of them have given up and started home in the belief that the story was now over, and in Matthew's account and in the second resurrection chapter of the fourth gospel, the disciples had gone back to Galilee. Only Mary of Magdala is portrayed in all of the canonical gospels as one who seeks, who weeps, who attempts to render service to the dead body of the one she has loved.

Dodd speaks of a "reflective, subtle, most delicate approach to the depths of human experience. This story never came out of any common stock of tradition; it has an arresting individuality."[26] Perhaps it is impossible to answer the real questions underlying this pericope but one question can be proposed. Is it possible that a woman wrote this segment of the fourth gospel? The gospel's multiple authorship is now generally acknowledged. Women are depicted prominently; at the wedding feast in Cana, at the well in Samaria, in Bethany when the woman anoints Jesus' feet, at the home of Martha and Mary, at the crucifixion. The only record of a male disciple at the crucifixion is found in the fourth gospel and, even there, he is not listed among those who are said to have been present. Women stood by that cross in all the gospel accounts. Even if one were to ignore the feminine elements so pronounced in this gospel, one is still left with the intensity, tenderness and personal nature of the encounter of Jesus with Mary of Magdala and the fact that this encounter is involved with a theology of resurrection and ascension.

In the fourth gospel, women are primary proclaimers of who Jesus is. The Samaritan woman returns to the village and tells her neighbors, "Come, see a man who told me all I ever did. Can this be the Christ?" (John 4:29); Martha is led in dialog by Jesus to the proclamation, "Yes, Lord, I have come to believe that you are the Messiah, the Son of God, the one who is coming into the world" (John 11:27); Mary of Magdala's role as primary messenger of resurrection fits the pattern of women who proclaim the realities of who Jesus is in this gospel. She is truly an apostle of the Lord. As Jerome Neyrey says, "She (Mary of Magdala) knows the most important things about Jesus in the Fourth Gospel, which indicates her special status as a receiver of heavenly revelations."[27]

CHAPTER 6

Women Leaders in the Ancient World

Some of the current interest in women's issues has developed into research into the roles women played in the ancient world. Previous to our day, the common understanding had been that women had no place in the political, economic and religious world and very little in the social world of the time. Important modifications have been made about that understanding due to renewed interest and modern methods of scholarship.

Some people today still cling to the belief that women of the ancient world were totally powerless and allowed themselves to remain so, that they were completely subject to men. Some others have attempted to take the opposite view and hold that women were powerful leaders who kept themselves free from male domination. Neither of these extreme views seems tenable. What is most probable is that some women in the ancient world were able to achieve positions of leadership and influence even though there were serious obstacles to such achievement. When this has been proven, can it be concluded that it was at least possible that Mary of Magdala could have been an influential leader in the early church?

Due to modern studies of inscriptional and archeological evidence and the scientific study of textual evidence, it is possible to discern that some women were acknowledged leaders, that some were important religious functionaries, that some were politically empowered in the ancient world. This occurred in spite of repressive laws and customs and a confusing legal system. It is possible to uncover some of this reality today despite the fact that most of the documentation available to us has been filtered through the lens of male authors.

The Roman World

One word sums up the situation of Roman women in the first century of the Christian era: ambivalence. During this century there was marked ambivalence in the application of Roman law and in the practice of Roman society. The Empire had begun to lose its aggressive drive for more extended hegemony and had taken on a demeanor somewhat more humane and peaceful. In addition, the vast geographical areas covered by Roman law were factors in mitigating the rigors of that law. For example, while Domitian, 81–96 CE, was demanding blind submission on the part of his officials and unlimited personal power in Rome and its environs, the provinces remained largely unaffected by this. The administration there worked efficiently and reliably.[1] In Rome, Stoic and Epicurean philosophers encouraged the education of women and advocated egalitarian woman-man relationships.[2] In fact, by the early second century, the education of women had become widespread enough so that in 116 CE Juvenal found it necessary to satirize it in a poem.[3]

There is strong evidence that, in the first century of the Christian era, women could inherit property, could be partners in legal contracts, could make wills, and could even initiate divorce.[4] Tacitus's *Annals* record that wives went with their husbands to their provinces and often took part in the administration of these provinces.[5] Organizations of women existed and exerted powerful influence. They even constituted guilds. "When women entered the senatorial order, the '*conventus matronum*' held an assembly. It was an ancient guild of religious origin," notes Friedlander.[6] Women were known to have devoted themselves to philosophy, to literature and to other cultural, social, political and religious pursuits.

During the first century CE laws of some consequence were ignored or interpreted in such a way that they lost their force. For example, in 19–18 BCE the "Julian Laws" attempted to restore family life, encourage marriage, discourage childlessness and even, possibly, encourage the subjugation of women. In 9 CE these original laws were supplemented by the Papian-Poppaean Law "in order to increase the penalties on celibacy and enrich the treasury."[7] Bachelors were forbidden to receive inheritances or legacies. The law "exempted women from marriage for one year after the death of a husband or six months after a divorce."[8] It also provided that widows and widowers between the ages of twenty and fifty had to remarry. However, the history of the time indicates that a gaping void existed between the laws and the observance of them. Blatant irony is found in the fact that the two officials who wrote the Papian-Poppaean Law, who caused the extension of the original law to be enacted and whose names are remembered precisely because of those laws, were bachelors at the time of the passage of their law and remained so until their deaths.[9]

These laws reflect the fact that the struggle to populate the empire was real, and that therefore childbearing was encouraged and promoted. If a woman bore several children, she could be rewarded by an increase in freedom. Thus a clause from one such law reads:

> Also to women who are unusually prolific, and who ought to be rewarded for the bearing of a certain number of offspring, I have granted exemption from work and sometimes even freedom, after they have raised many children....[10]

Obviously the price of a woman's freedom was high. However, the two examples show a creeping leniency about the enforcement of Roman law. The laws seem to have been enforced and circumvented with almost equal ease.

Another example of the oppression of women can be found in the Roman practice of *tutela* or guardianship. Under law, "the wife was still regarded merely as a piece of property completely under the control of her husband."[11] The practice was intended to keep women totally in subjection to husbands or other male relatives. Legal fictions and varieties of interpretation were introduced in efforts to avoid the terms of the law that were often impossible to implement. Fairly often fathers and husbands found ways to leave their inheritances under the control of wives or daughters—for example, by assigning as *tutela* a friend who did not interfere with the independent woman, or by simply ignoring the legislation and allowing the woman to take care of her own financial affairs. It has even been shown that women could be legally freed from guardianship. Lewis quotes the following:

> ...laws have been made, Most Eminent Prefect, which empower women who are honored with the right of three children to be independent and act without a guardian in whatever business they transact, especially those who know how to write....

Or another example:

> Request for release from guardianship from Aurelia Thaisous.[12]

The ambivalence about roles permitted to women was masculine in origin and in practice. Men acquiesced in the formulation of laws that made freedom for women impossible. Yet they abetted women in their efforts to achieve some independent status. One cause was the ease with which laws were generally ignored—the beginning, we now see, of the collapse of the Roman legal system. A further contributing factor to the ambivalence was, without doubt, the fact that women simply would not submit to their legal role of subordination. Historical records bear out the fact that some women achieved respectability, status and power and that men acquiesced either through good will, or through inability to change the situation, or even possibly because they recognized that they could not function adequately without the women.

Hellenistic Circles

Historians seem to agree that Hellenistic women had achieved an even more remarkable degree of legal and social independence than Roman women. As Sir James Donaldson has written:

> Especially in Asia Minor did women display public activity. Their generosity took the most various forms, even to bestowing considerable sums on each citizen in their own cities. They erected baths and gymnasia, adorned temples, put up statues, and contributed in every way to the enjoyment of their fellow-countrymen. They often presided at the public games or over great religious ceremonies, having been regularly appointed to this position, and they paid the expenses incurred in these displays. In consequence of this, they received the most marked distinctions and were elected to the highest magistracies. They also held priesthoods, and several of them obtained the highest priesthood of Asia—perhaps the greatest honor that could be paid to anyone.[13]

This description of the position of women in Asia Minor may sound a bit too enthusiastic about the role they played in religious, civic, recreational and political affairs, but it can be supported by further evidence from inscriptions:

Senate and people honoured Aurelia Harmasta, also Tertia, daughter of Medon and chaste wife of Aremas, of the highest birth, who acted as priestess of Hera the Queen, and as demiurge, and as chief priest, and did all that was usual on such occasions.

Aur. Arternianus Deleitrianus Artemus, her husband, erected the statue.[14]

A conclusive body of evidence exists which indicates that the economic, political, social and religious lives of Hellenistic women in Asia Minor in the first century of the Christian era were open to significant exercise of independence and power.

It is easily proven that women could, and did, obtain rights and functioned in meaningful ways in the society of Asia Minor, but it is important to recognize that they did so through struggle, through paying high prices for elementary rights, and through courageous actions of exercising personal freedom when legal freedom was denied them. At a time when they were achieving political, social, financial and religious freedom, they were still legally bound by repressive measures, such as laws compelling them to marry, and by the institution of *tutela* which still subjected all women living in the empire to the financial control of men. Some women moved comfortably in whatever circles they chose to frequent and made significant contributions in their locality. This ambivalence undergirds much of the life of the first century.

The Jewish Milieu

We possess little evidence for the situation in the Jewish world of the first century CE. Study of this time and place is seriously disadvantaged because of the absence of written documents. However, evidence does exist from inscriptions and epigraphs, from archeological finds, and from later writings that reflect life in first-century Palestine. As van der Horst has noted:

> One of the most interesting aspects of our epitaphs as far as women are concerned is that of the titles or functions assigned to women in the religious communities. There are some 20 inscriptions in which women bear titles like "head of the synagogue," "mother of the synagogue," "elder," or "leader." Until recently most scholars assumed that women had no positions of leadership in the ancient synagogue. Therefore, they interpreted such titles borne by women as purely honorific and not functional. Over the last decade opinions have begun to change on this subject.[15]

Bernadette Brooten has amassed a significant body of evidence from inscriptions. The materials she investigates date from 27 BCE to 500 CE and come from many parts of the Near East. Her thesis is: "Women served as leaders in a number of synagogues during the Roman and Byzantine periods."[16] Brooten believes that evidence supporting her thesis is irrefutable and that, since most of it has been known for many years, it is the interpretation of it that has obscured the reality. She blames this blindness on the use of circular reasoning and demonstrates how misleading that has been. Even if one were to find fault with Brooten's interpretation of one or several of the inscriptions, the overall effect of the total body of inscriptional evidence that she has gathered has to be, as she states, that women were engaged in leadership roles in the synagogues.

An element of the discussion that Brooten excluded completely is the belief that women were so segregated from Jewish worship in the first century that they were relegated to balconies. She employs the results of extensive archeological excavations of Palestinian synagogues to refute this false theory. First-century synagogues were not built with balconies.[17]

It was necessary, earlier in the study, to examine in detail the single reference to Mary of Magdala outside of the crucifixion, burial and resurrection stories.[18] The passage is relevant here because it speaks of women who were able to use their own resources to assist voluntary associations.

> Afterwards, he journeyed from one town and village to another, preaching and proclaiming the good news of the kingdom of God. Accompanying him were the Twelve and some women who had been cured of evil spirits and infirmities, Mary, called Magdalene, from whom seven demons had gone out, Joanna, the wife of Herod's servant Chuza, Susanna, and many others who provided for them out of their resources.[19]

The words translated "out of their resources" mean literally, "of their property." Obviously, these women were identified as donors to the work of Jesus and his followers. Horsley mentions two examples of inscriptional evidence that show women as principal donors to the synagogue and mentions that many other similar inscriptions exist.[20] Brooten lists forty-three such inscriptions. The most complete inscription, which comes from the first century BCE, is most resistant to misinterpretation:

> The building was erected by Julia Severa, P. Tyrronius Klados, the head-for-life of the synagogue and Lucius, son of Lucius, head of the synagogues, and Publius Zotikos, archon, restored it with their own funds and the money which had been deposited....[21]

Horsley cites an equally clear example:

> Tation, daughter of Straton, son of Empedon, having built (or furnished) the meeting room and the precinct of the hypaithos at her expense, bestowed a favor on the Jews. The synagogue of the

Jews honored Tation, daughter of Straton, son of Empedon, with
a gold crown and a seat of honor.[22]

It is clear that Julia Severa and Tation, daughter of Straton, by their
own largesse, built synagogues. It is impossible to interpret these
passages as intending anything else. These passages enable us to
read Luke 8:1-3 as possibly reflecting a historical situation.

Another inscription, which can be dated around 55 BCE, was
found in Cyrenicia, a considerable distance from Palestine to be
sure, but part of the same cultural milieu. It reads: "Isidora, daughter (or wife) of Seraphon, 5 drachmas. Zosime, daughter (or wife) of
Terpolius, 3 drachmas."[23] The amounts are small but not insignifi-
cant and the implications are large. Women contributed, in their
own names, to the building and upkeep of synagogues. In the
works of Pieter van der Horst, G. H. R. Horsley, Bernadette Brooten
and others, there is convincing evidence that Roman and Jewish
women, who were in control of their own finances, contributed to
the upkeep of religious institutions. The Lukan reference fits this
pattern since it indicates that Jewish women, in their own right,
could contribute to the material support of Jesus and his band of
disciples of which they were a part.

Another title found in inscriptions and epigraphs is "official
of the synagogue," in Greek, *archisunagogon.* The word is translated "leader of the synagogue" in the New Revised Standard and
several other versions of the Bible. It is found in an inscription
already cited.[24] It appears in Mark 5:22: "One of the synagogue officials [leaders] named Jairus," and in the similar passage in Luke
8:41, "Jairus, an official [leader] of the synagogue." In these cases
and in other uses (Mark 5:35, 36, 38, Luke 13:14, Acts 13:15, 18:8, 17)
the same word, *archisunagogon,* is used. It seems safe to assume
that the office of official or leader of the synagogue included active
administration of the congregation, financial management, and

even teaching. Brooten and van der Horst both discuss inscriptions where the word is used to describe women.[25] Brooten includes one such inscription that dates from the second century CE. It was found in Smyrna.

> Rufina, a Jewess, head of the synagogue, built this tomb for her freed slaves and the slaves raised in her house. No one else has the right to bury anyone [here]. If someone should dare to do so, he or she will pay 1500 denars to the sacred treasury and 1000 denars to the Jewish people. A copy of this inscription has been placed in the [public] archives.[26]

In addition to the identification of Rufina as Jewess and "head of the synagogue," the inscription makes clear that Rufina had the right to free her slaves, to impose a fine, to control her own finances, and to cause an order to be inscribed in the public archives. The inscription rings with authority and power as well as concern for the slaves.

Pieter van der Horst comments upon the importance of another inscription from Crete that dates from the Imperial Age: "Sophia of Gortyn, elder and leader of the synagogue of Kissamos [lies] here. The memory of the righteous [woman] be forever. Amen."[27] There are later inscriptions that also refer to a woman as head or leader of the synagogue. It would not be difficult to assume that Mary of Magdala could have held a similar position. Another title that occurs regularly is "elder," often in the form *presbutera*, clearly a feminine form. Brooten concludes that the title seems likely to have referred to membership in a council of elders. Van der Horst lists eight such inscriptions from the first century CE onwards and from a variety of locations.[28]

The title "mother of the synagogue" occurs in two Greek inscriptions and in two Latin inscriptions. One woman is even referred to as *pateressa*. These evidences scattered throughout Asia Minor and Italy raise many questions about the role women actually played in these parts of the Roman world, not the least of which is their role as scholars. The amassed evidence of the epigraphs viewed objectively is clear: women headed synagogues, were important presences there, performed administrative duties there and exerted some power in public life. Horsley's findings indicate that women were held in high regard.[29] Van der Horst even suggests that women may, in some instances, have been responsible for the cult in the synagogue.[30]

Even more startling may be the three ancient Jewish inscriptions Brooten lists in which the word *hiereia* (priest) or *hieressa* is used of a woman. The clearest inscription bearing the title *hieressa* was found in lower Egypt and dates to the first century BCE:

> O Marin (Marion), priest, good friend to all, causing pain to no one and friendly to your neighbors, farewell! She died at the age of approximately fifty years, in the third year of Caesar [Augustus] on the thirteenth day of Payni [July 7, 28 BCE].[31]

Brooten concludes her discussion of these references to women as priests with the cogent comment: "If the three inscriptions had come from another Graeco-Roman religion, no scholar would have thought of arguing that 'priest' does not mean priest."[32]

There was a clearly defined role for women as deacons in the earliest days of the church. In Romans 16:1, Paul names Phoebe *diakonon*, deacon. In First Timothy a series of regulations about the conduct of deacons includes the women (1 Tim 3:10). Horsley quotes Pliny's having written that "in Bithnyia under Trajan, there were female deacons."[33] A stele has been found near Jerusalem, on the Mount of Olives, on which is inscribed, "Here lies the slave and bride of Christ, Sophia, deacon, the second Phiobe, who fell asleep in peace on the 21st of the month during the 11th indiction."[34] Horsley adds an impressive list of inscriptions referring to female deacons. This evidence, once again, is extensive and compelling. To paraphrase Bernadette Brooten, in no other situation would anyone question that the word deacon means deacon.

Whatever modern study of epigraphic and inscriptional evidence is used, the evidence is overwhelming that some women did function in leadership roles in and around the first century of the Christian era. Horsley shows that the texts provide a continuity of evidence for women office-holders in the church.[35] Powerful women were described in terms that indicate leadership, prestige, authority and admiration.

Over the centuries a process of interpreting the evidence occurred that can now be seen as seriously flawed. Misinterpretations resulted from three techniques: deciding that titles were honorific for women but not for men, deciding that women only received titles as reflected glory from their husbands, deciding that the titles cannot mean what they say because it is known that women could not hold such offices. All three of these techniques employ the circular reasoning obvious in the last one: the titles cannot mean what they say because it is known that women did not hold such offices.

It would seem more honest and more scholarly to accept the massed evidence that some women did hold important offices in the ancient world, in synagogues and in Roman institutions. Horsley calls biblical scholarship to task by asking a question whose answer is all too obvious. He quotes an inscription and then comments:

> "As for your domestic virtues, loyalty (to our marriage), obedience, courteousness, easy good nature, your assiduous woolworking, reverence for the gods, without superstition, attire not

designed for attracting attention, modest refinement...." Has this inscription been picked up and drawn upon by Biblical Studies for the light it has to shed upon the marriage relationship of a Roman couple of 12 BCE?[36]

He calls our attention to the failure of those involved in biblical studies to recognize the high esteem in which many wives were held. He asks the important question: Why this failure?

If it is possible to look at the evidence without preconceived notions, it can be stated quite unequivocally that it was possible for someone like Mary of Magdala to function in one or several important roles in the early church. It is not a viable assertion to claim that Christian women whose backgrounds were in Judaism would have been unable to bridge the gap to leadership roles in the church.

In the Mishnah

There is an almost total lack of written documentation from Palestine during the formative years of the Christian church. Some investigation of that period of Hebrew history has been accomplished by retrojecting material from the Mishnah to the ages when its contents were being formulated. Whatever historicity that procedure might possess, some of the thinking, customs, and practices of first-century Judaism may be discerned behind the regulations of the Mishnah.

The Mishnah as we know it today evolved in two different eras of the second century of the Christian era. It reflects a way of life that had developed over many centuries of Hebrew history. It is as authoritative about life in the first century as it is about life in the second century. The Mishnah is a collection of laws, customs, "traditions of the elders," explanations. It is firmly based on Torah and contains the written expression of the *halakoth* or oral laws of

Judaism. The final compilation is usually dated between 160 CE and 200 CE.

There are six orders in the Mishnah of which the third is entitled *nashim,* women. "Women's importance in the mishnaic world is highlighted by the fact that the Mishnah's redactors (or some later editor) chose to name one of its six sections, the Division of Women," Judith Romney Wegner points out. "The absence of a corresponding Division of Men reflects the fact that in patriarchies men make rules about women, but women do not make rules about men."[37.]

In spite of the optimism of some commentators, the role ascribed to women in the Mishnah is hardly one of affirmation—at least that is what has been taught over the intervening centuries. Eugene Lipman makes this distinction:

> First, women were not considered inferior beings, or slaves or chattels. Woman's major—if not dominant—role in society was clearly recognized by Jewish tradition. All limitations on woman's rights in the synagogue and the home were based on realistic factors in the life of the female—chiefly her household duties and her state of ritual cleanliness.[38]

It is not easy to reconcile this thesis from Lipman's work on the Mishnah with the evidence of the written mishnoth. There are many passages that seem clearly repressive, at least by modern standards. For example:

> R. Eliezer says: If any man gives his daughter a knowledge of the Law, it is as though he taught her lechery.[39]

A passage quoted by Herbert Danby asserts that a man must be saved alive sooner than a woman, and his lost property must be restored sooner than hers.[40] Still two more examples:

Jose b. Johanan of Jerusalem said: Let thy house be opened wide and let the needy be members of thy household; and talk not much with womankind. They said this of a man's own wife: how much more of his fellow's wife! Hence the Sages have said: He that talks much with womankind brings evil upon himself and neglects the study of the Law and at the last will inherit Gehenna.[41]

If a woman went in to bring out bread to a poor man and she came out and found him standing beside loaves of Heave-offering (so, too, if a woman went out and found her neighbor raking coals under a cooking pot in which was Heave-offering) Rabbi Akimbo declares it unclean, but the Sages clean. R. Eliza b. Pila said: But why did R. Akimbo declare it unclean and the Sages clean?—because women are gluttonous; for a woman is suspected of uncovering her neighbor's cooking pot to know what she is cooking.[42]

These are representative of many such passages. One maintains that a woman may not bring a bill of divorce. However, the court can force her husband to give her a bill of divorce. "The use of various formulas permits husband and wife alike to influence the divorce process by controlling the time or place of the wife's receipt of her writ," says Wegner.[43]

In spite of this dominant repressive tone, there are cogent reasons for modifying the belief that women were totally subservient and without rights in the society reflected in the Mishnah. It is easy to find other passages that clearly intended to safeguard the rights of men and women equally. For example:

If defects arose in the husband, they may not compel him to put away his wife. R. Simeon b. Gameliel said: this applies only to the lesser defects, but for the greater defects they can compel him to put away his wife.[44]

A man may betroth a woman either by his own act or by that of his agent; and a woman may become betrothed either by her own act or by that of her agent.[45]

There are many other passages that excuse women from various religious observances because they are required to be elsewhere or are doing such necessary things as household chores. Some of the restrictions placed on women in the Mishnah were intended to safeguard the time and energy of the housewife.

Women never achieved equal rights under Jewish law. However, what light can be gleaned from the Mishnah raises the suspicion that total repression was not the reality. There were apparently some efforts to afford women equal rights, or at least some power of determination especially in regard to marriage contracts and household duties.

It is not possible to use the Mishnah to find a reflection of the actual lives of Jewish people in the first and second centuries of the Christian era. Even though this sometimes has been attempted, the facts are that it is extremely difficult to decide what historical value we should attach to any of the traditions recorded in the Mishnah. The Mishnah reflects only the opinions of the Pharisaic party, not those of the Sadducees, or any other group, nor does it necessarily reflect the actual life of the time. Before and after 70 CE there was no strong central structure that could or would enforce regulations, especially in geographically distant areas. The Mishnah betrays a tendency to exploit every aspect of every issue in a fine display of intellectual resourcefulness. The reality of everyday living might well have been, and probably was, quite unlike the picture that can be discerned in the Mishnah.

The only conclusion that can be drawn after this very cursory examination is that it is not clear what role women played. Women had some rights and privileges under mishnaic law but there is no evidence that these laws determined everyday existence for most Jewish people of the first century. Nonetheless, it remains true that Jewish women have never achieved a high degree of equal rights. Judith Romney Wegner came to this interesting conclusion: "When I began to see that I needed to focus more on the control of women's sexuality and procreativity than on the usual economic questions, the distinction between women as chattel and woman as person became stunningly clear."[46] This illustrates the need for careful distinctions about the roles of Jewish women in the ancient world from yet another perspective.

This chapter began with a question. Is it possible that Mary of Magdala could have achieved an important leadership role in the church of the first century? Clearly, it is possible. We have evidence that women functioned in important capacities: political, social, economic and religious. The interpretation of the Mishnah, which has been used to indicate that women were treated as property, even as chattels, has to be replaced by the understanding that whatever else mishnaic law portrays, the Mishnah cannot be used as proof that women were kept in subjection.

From inscriptional and epigraphic evidence we can conclude that, indeed, it could have been that a woman like Mary of Magdala achieved an important leadership role in the early Christian church. From archeological evidence it can be concluded that women were not relegated to balconies in first-century synagogues. From textual evidence, it can be concluded that the testimony of the Mishnah is inconclusive about the role of women in the first century of the Christian era.

CHAPTER 7

Women in the Apocryphal and Canonical Literature

In the Apocrypha

It has been established that it was possible for women to achieve leadership roles in the early church. It remains to examine the probability that Mary of Magdala was a woman who could have risen to a leadership role in that early church. Could it be true that Mary of Magdala, whose name for so many centuries has been associated with prostitution, could have been a prominent leader in the early days of the Christian church? There is much evidence to suggest that she was, indeed, an important leader in that church. Were the history of the past twenty centuries different from what we know it to be, it would be sufficient to establish the fact that she was an important personage in the early church by pointing out that Mary of Magdala alone is mentioned in all four canonical gospels as the primary recipient of the message of resurrection, and is written of in most of the apocryphal gospels. The tendency was, of course, to move in the opposite direction and to paint her as the "sinful woman." It is important to examine the literature of the first centuries of the Christian era to discern what role Mary of Magdala actually played.

There is ample evidence of an important role played by Mary of Magdala in the apocryphal literature and, it should be pointed out at the outset, that literature was not all gnostic. Walter Bauer wrote that "it is impossible neatly to divide the Christian writings known to us down to the year 200 between orthodoxy and heresy."[1] Nonetheless, there was, in the early church, a clear condemnation of gnostic writings. This condemnation includes some works cited in this chapter, such as "The Dialog of the Savior," "The Gospel of Philip," the *Sophia Jesus Christi, Pistils Sophia,* and "The Gospel of Mary." One blatantly anti-gnostic writing exists in the *Epistula Apostolorum.*[2] A second writing relevant to the thesis is "The Gospel of Peter"[3] which cannot be classified as either gnostic or anti-gnostic, since it contains elements of both orientations. References to Mary of Magdala are prominent in these and other writings from the early Christian centuries. It has been claimed that the "Gnostic Gospels" were written by women, hence, they were not reliable. This is one reason that so many of those gospels were classified as gnostic regardless of their content or orientation.

The *Epistula Apostolorum* is clearly an anti-gnostic document, especially in its second part.[4] In form, it consists of a postresurrection dialog between Jesus and some of his disciples. The provenance is probably Egypt sometime in the early second century of the Christian era. The eleven apostles are listed individually and they tell the story of the crucifixion, burial and resurrection of Jesus that is based upon the same traditions as those that underlie the synoptic accounts. The resurrection narrative contains the story of Martha and Mary and Sarah going to the tomb. Sarah's identity is unknown and her name appearing here indicates how easily names are inserted into ancient documents.

Since the discovery of the Nag Hammadi documents in 1945 a complete Ethiopic text of the *Epistula Apostolorum* and a fragmentary Coptic text have been available. Mary Magdalene appears in both. The Ethiopic text reads: "... and was buried in the place called *garanejo (kraniou)* to which three women came: Sarah, Martha, and Mary Magdalen."[5] The text goes on to say that after the description of their mourning and the first appearance of the risen Lord to them, Mary and her friends went to the apostles and told them that Jesus had risen. The apostles refused to believe them:

> And Mary came to us and told us. And we said to her, "what have we to do with you, O woman? He that is dead and buried, can he then live?" And we did not believe her, that our Savior had risen from the dead.[6]

Sarah was then dispatched with the same message with the same result. Finally, the Lord said to Mary and to her sisters, "Let us go to them."[7] The primacy of Mary as leader and bearer of the news of the risen Jesus is beyond doubt here. The Coptic version has Martha as the first messenger and Mary as the second, but the response of Jesus is again "to Mary and to her sisters." The belief, the women's willingness to proclaim it, and Mary's leadership all are in strong contrast to the lingering disbelief of the apostles. Whatever the meaning of this narrative, it is true that the writer of this strongly anti-gnostic early account is very conscious of the role of Mary of Magdala as primary witness to the news of resurrection, and that she is commissioned to carry that news to the disciples who are reluctant to believe.

A second important source of information about the esteem in which Mary of Magdala was held in the early church is the "Gospel of Peter." Its source seems to have been western Syria, probably in the early second century. It is within the realm of possibility that the pertinent passages about Mary are as old as, or even older than, those in the canonical gospels. Says Helmut Koester: "In a number of instances the 'Gospel of Peter' contains features that can be traced back to a stage in the development of the passion narrative and the story of the empty tomb which is older than that known by the canonical gospels."[8]

The "Gospel of Peter" concludes with a resurrection account that is closely related to the empty-tomb narrative in Mark 16:1–8. The "Gospel of Peter" is somewhat more realistic than Mark's account because the three errors the women make in Mark (seeking the body of Jesus, wishing to anoint it and worrying about who will roll back the stone) are modified in the "Gospel of Peter," where the women wish to weep openly as they had been afraid to do "for fear of the Jews." They have formulated an alternate plan should they be unable to roll away the stone:

> For the stone was great—and we fear lest anyone see us. And if we cannot do so, let us at least put down at the entrance what we bring as a memorial of him and let us weep and lament until we have again gone home.[9]

Even the young man who awaits them in the sepulcher offers a second option:

> Wherefore are ye come? Whom seek ye? Not him that was crucified? He is risen and gone. But if ye believe not, stoop this way and see the place where he lay, for he is not here. For he is risen and is gone thither whence he was sent.[10]

The women flee in fear and the narrative ends with a cryptic picture of the disciples returning to their occupation as fishermen.

Here again, it is clear that Mary Magdalene is the central character and the leader of the action. She is designated "a woman disciple of the Lord," and it is she who takes her sisters with her. The details that differ from those in the canonical gospels are realistic concerns, such as their desire to weep over the body at the entrance to the tomb as they had been unable to do before. They face the possibility that they may not be able to roll back the stone, in contrast to the Markan account, where they worry about who will roll it back for them. Mary leads the women and proposes alternate purposes for the visit to the tomb. This gospel's final comment, that the women fled in fear, is no more enigmatic here than in Mark 16:8, "They said nothing to anyone for they were afraid."

The Coptic "Gospel of Thomas," which was translated from the Greek, can probably be placed in Syria or Palestine around the end of the first century of the Christian era. This gospel contains many obviously gnostic elements but can not be considered a totally gnostic work. "The influence of gnostic theology is clearly present in the Gospel of Thomas, though it is not possible to ascribe the work to any particular school or sect."[11] The saying that has been designated number 21 by scholars reads: "Mary said to Jesus, 'Whom are your disciples like?'"[12] The question provides Jesus the occasion to speak of ownership of land and protection from thieves. Logion 114, the last saying of this gospel, reads:

> Simon Peter said to them, "Let Mary leave us, for women are not worthy of life." Jesus said, "I myself shall lead her in order to make her male, so that she too may become a living spirit resembling you males. For every woman who will make herself male will enter the Kingdom of Heaven."[13]

This logion is certainly not a claim for the equality of women but it makes a statement that, like it or not, is still basic to much "religious" thinking. Woman can only be acceptable in the kingdom to the extent that she becomes male. The point is not to evaluate the sexual relationship herein portrayed, but to recognize the importance of Mary of Magdala whom Jesus will make male because she is to become part of the kingdom of heaven. It is to be noted that the conflict with Peter is overt and the center of the action. It probably reflects something of the situation of the churches at the time of the writing of this gospel. Peter was a leader in competition with Mary of Magdala or else followers of Peter were in competition with followers of Mary. The redactor of the "Gospel of Peter" clearly places Mary in a position higher than that of Peter.

Another document from the late first or early second century, from Syria or near Syria, also containing gnosticizing tendencies is "The Dialog of the Savior." It employs the gnostic device of expanding sayings into dialogs. Three disciples are in dialog with Jesus: Matthew, Judas and Mariam. The document, as we have it today, is complex in sources and in structure but not in theological concern. The theological statement is very clear: the kingdom is to come and yet is here. The dialog—actually expanded sayings—forms a coherent basis and probably was an original document to which much has been added. In one place Mary says: "Tell me Lord, why have I come to this place, to benefit or to suffer loss?" The Lord responds: "Because you (sing.) reveal the greatness of the revealer."[14] Mary is held up as the bearer of the revelation. In this statement, and throughout the dialog, she is set above the other two disciples.

Just previous to this passage, Mary speaks with Judas:

> Mariam said, "Thus about the wickedness of each day and the laborer being worthy of his food, and the disciple resembling his teacher." This word she spoke as a woman who knew the All.[15]

From that point until the end of the discussion, Mary is the leader. She speaks about wickedness, the laborer earning his food, the disciple resembling the teacher. She asks about the purpose of her being with Jesus, her own relationship with truth, the origin of all things, the mystery of truth, the mustard seed and the problems of dissolution.

Elaine Pagels has commented upon the section of "The Dialog of the Savior" which deals with the statement of Matthew that the works of femaleness must be destroyed:

The target is not woman, but the power of sexuality....Mary Magdalene, praised as "the woman who knew the All," stands among three disciples who receive Jesus' commands. She, along with Judas and Matthew, rejects the "works of femaleness" that is, apparently, the activities of intercourse and procreation.[16]

As a "woman who knew the All," Mary of Magdala was raised to such a peak of importance in "The Dialog of the Savior" there can be little doubt that she held importance for the community from which this tradition has risen. It is especially important that Mary was praised above the two male disciples who participate in the dialog. It is also significant that some scholars believe that, "in its theological themes, 'The Dialog of the Savior' is also an important predecessor of the Johannine theology since it discusses the problems of a realized eschatology for the Christian church."[17] One aspect of the realized eschatology of the fourth gospel, that which concerns the place of women, has been discussed above.[18]

One strongly gnostic writing from the Nag Hammadi Library is "The Gospel of Philip." Egypt in the second or early third century is the most likely provenance. Many aspects of this gospel are problematic and require extensive work. However, there is no doubt about the meaning of this sentence: "There were three who always walked with the Lord: Mary his mother and her sister and Magdalene the one who is called his companion (koinonas)."[19] Jesus' mother and her sister are included as blood relations. Mary of Magdala is included because of the importance of her role in the early church. It has been pointed out that this identical group of women is found at the crucifixion scene in the fourth gospel.

Wilhelm Schneemelcher, in his introduction to the document *Sophia Jesu Christi,* says that a dialog occurs between Jesus and a gathering of holy men and women in a form familiar to gnostic hearers. The men are listed by name: Philip, Thomas, Bartholomew,

Matthew, the Twelve, and "Mary (Magdalene) the only one of the holy women present who is expressly named."[20] The structure of the work is highly artificial as the disciples take turns proposing questions. However, the final, far-reaching question is assigned to Mary, "Holy Lord, your disciples, whence came they, and where do they go, and (what) should they do here?"[21] Mary is clearly on an equal footing with Matthew, Philip and Thomas. She dominates the end of the dialog as she did in the "Dialog of the Savior."

It is important to bear in mind the impact of this accumulated body of evidence. Mary of Magdala appears repeatedly with the chosen disciples; she is given the leading role in the dialogs; she is singled out as a primary disciple; she is, more than once, in direct conflict with Peter from which conflict she emerges as the stronger character.

There are other instances of Mary's role as leader found in the literature of the early church. In the *Pistis Sophia*, Mary proposes 39 of the 45 questions asked. Scholars are uncertain about the provenance of this document. Equally elusive is the identification of fragments connected with the name Bartholomew. In one such fragment, "The Gospel of Bartholomew," an entire section is devoted to a narrative of the resurrection. Mary is the chief character. Jesus speaks to her, "whom he favors with words of blessing and then charges her to inform his disciples of His Resurrection. Mary asks for Jesus' blessing, and receives the promise that she will be with Christ in his Kingdom."[22]

Mary's dominant presence in the resurrection narratives continues into the third century. In one of the variations of the "Acts of Pilate" she is involved in the denunciation of Pilate: "Mary Magdalene said, weeping,...'Who shall make this known unto all the world? I will go alone to Rome unto Caesar: I will show him what evil Pilate hath done, consenting to the wicked Jews.'"[23]

From this same age comes the "Gospel of Mary." In this document Mary is called upon to console, strengthen and enlighten the disciples who are thoroughly distraught at Jesus' departure from them. Peter says to Mary, "Sister, we know that the Savior loved you more than the rest of women. Tell us the words of the Savior which you remember—which you know (but) we do not nor have we heard them."[24] And Mary explains her vision of the risen Lord. At the end of this scene, Andrew raises an objection because the teachings Mary has relayed are strange. Peter then asks why Jesus would "speak privately with a woman (and) not openly to us? Are we to turn about and listen to her? Did he prefer her to us?"[25] Levi comes to Mary's rescue and declares that the Savior knew Mary better than the disciples knew her, and that was why he loved her more than he loved them. The dimensions of the struggle between the followers of Peter and the followers of Mary of Magdala are again evident.

In addition to her clearly defined role as primary bearer of the message of resurrection, there is a long history of inclusion of Mary of Magdala in the struggle to understand and live according to the mystery of the resurrection. Her prominence in documentary evidence, which lasted well into the third century, goes far beyond the admittedly narrow confines of the gnostic literature. Perhaps it is understating the case to label Mary of Magdala an important apostle of the early church; perchance, she should be called the primary apostle.

In the Canonical Literature

The probability that Mary of Magdala was an important or primary leader in the early church must also be examined in the New Testament writings other than the gospels. An examination of the texts in which Mary is named will constitute the major part of this study. The roles of other women in the New Testament will be sketched briefly.

Even without the legitimate claims of those proposing a "feminist hermeneutic," with all the valuable insights it can provide, it is still eminently possible to discern that women in the New Testament were important leaders in their communities, using traditional exegetical tools. Since women are known to have exercised important leadership roles in the first-century church, it is even more probable that someone of Mary Magdalene's stature could have been an important leader in that church.

Women held a variety of leadership roles in the early church, if the canonical documents reflect anything of a historical reality. Their exercise of leadership seems to have been taken for granted since there is no comment upon it in any of the passages where women are mentioned in leadership roles.

Paul referred to various women as his coworkers. The Greek word *synergos* is normally translated "coworker." It may also be translated "associate" or "coadjutor."[26] *Synergos* is used many times in Paul's letters and always has the same meanings. The coworkers are those who lead the community in Paul's absence. They are held responsible for the activities of the group and for remaining in contact with Paul. They teach and preach and conduct worship. They are active in spreading the gospel.

In Romans 16:3, Paul sends greetings to "Prisca and Aquila, my coworkers in Christ Jesus." It is to be noted here that, as Paul sends greetings to the couple, Prisca's name comes first. This is repeated in Acts 18:18 and 18:26. Normally, the husband's name would be first. Since Paul reverses the normal order, the assumption is that Prisca somehow preceded her husband in importance. Thus, Prisca was also acknowledged by Paul and by the author of Acts to be a prominent leader in the early Christian community.

In the fourth chapter of the letter to the Philippians, Paul requests a peacemaking between Euodia and Syntyche: "I urge Euodia and I urge Syntyche to come to a mutual understanding in the Lord. Yes, and I ask you also, my true yokemate, to help them, for they have struggled at my side in promoting the gospel, along with Clement and my other coworkers" (Phil 4:2–3). Euodia and Syntyche were significant enough as leaders in that community that their disagreement had become known and that it posed a serious problem for the whole group. Acts 16:14–15 describes the origin of the community at Philippi in the conversion and activism of "a woman named Lydia...[who] listened and the Lord opened her heart to pay attention to what Paul was saying. After she and her household had been baptized...." Feminine leadership in that church was taken for granted—no comment on it was deemed necessary.

There were other women leaders in the Christian churches in Paul's time. In addition to Lydia's contribution, Acts describes Peter's going to the "house of Mary, the mother of John who is called Mark, where there were many people gathered in prayer" (Acts 12:12). Paul's letter to Philemon speaks of "Apphia, our sister, to Archippus our fellow soldier, and to the church at your house" (Phlm 2). In the letter to the Colossians, Paul sends greetings to "Nympha and to the church in her house" (Col 4:15). Prisca and Aquila are also mentioned among those who have a church in their house (1 Cor 16:19). The real meanings and mechanisms of the house churches must be studied within Paul's overall understanding of community and the roles of the members of the community.[27] The freedom and responsibility of each member of a house church was certainly part of Paul's conception of house church—this colors the understandings we derive about leadership roles. The fact remains, however, that Paul identifies house churches by the name of the person in whose home that church gathers and, in the examples cited, women are identified as those who assembled a church.

Paul's letter to the Romans has this greeting: "Greet Andronicus and Junia, my relatives and my fellow prisoners; they are prominent among the apostles and they were in Christ before me" (Rom 16:7).

The term "apostle" has been examined.[28] There are variations in its uses, especially when used in conjunction with the terms "disciple" or in "the Twelve." Paul uses the term "apostle" sparingly except when justifying his own role as apostle as he does in, "For as I see it, God has exhibited us apostles as the last of all" (1 Cor 4:9); "do we not have the right to take along a Christian wife, as do the rest of the apostles?" (1 Cor 9:5); "For I am the least of the apostles, not fit to be called an apostle, because I persecuted the church of God" (1 Cor 15:9), and in a variety of other passages. Paul fairly consistently refers to himself as one called to be an apostle. He also uses the term to refer to the original group in Jerusalem, "nor did I go up to Jerusalem to those who were apostles before me" (Gal 1:17). Paul's practice in using the term "apostle" makes its application to Andronicus and Junia significant. Paul does not restrict the term to "Twelve" who were appointed by Jesus. Junia is a feminine name and Paul is acknowledging her role as apostle and a prominent one at that. It would seem strange indeed if he had used one word for two people but intended it to have a different meaning for the woman than it obviously held for the man. Paul recognizes Junia as apostle and leader in the early church.

Probably the clearest reference to a woman leader in the Pauline churches is found at the beginning of chapter 16 of Romans, "I commend to you Phoebe our sister, who is also minister (*diakonon*) of the church at Cenchreae...for she has been a benefactor to many and to me as well" (Rom 16:1–2). In Phoebe's case, the Greek word *diakonon* is often translated "minister." In the case of Stephen (Acts 7) and Philip (Acts 8) it is translated "deacon." There is no reason to believe that *diakonon* means something different when Paul uses it of a woman and there is no reason to assume that Phoebe as deacon ministered only to women. Paul clearly asserts that she is "deacon of the church at Cenchreae." To limit her role to the service of women misinterprets Paul's words.

The English word "benefactor" is often used as the translation for *prostatis*. The Greek word means, in addition to benefactor, helper or patron. In First Thessalonians it is translated "who are over you in the Lord" (1 Thess 5:12). The word is used in participle form twice in First Timothy and there it means to manage one's household and to preside well in the roles of preaching and teaching. The "ordained" role of deacon had not become known in Phoebe's time, but the role of servant, benefactor and presider and manager of a group seems to have been well understood in the early church. To recognize Phoebe as deacon and benefactor is to recognize her as a leader of the church at Cenchreae who managed temporal affairs, who taught and who preached in that church.

In the narratives of the early church, women were, without comment, named prophets: "He had four virgin daughters gifted with prophecy" (Acts 21:9). They are named as teachers of male leaders: "He (Apollos) began to speak boldly in the synagogue; but when Priscilla and Aquila heard him, they took him aside and explained to him the Way more accurately" (Acts 18:26).

Women were known as performers of works of service and charity. It must be recognized that roles as we know them today did not exist at all in these early churches. The goal, both of Paul and in Acts, was an ideal community in which all responsibility was shared equally. Not many churches achieved the goal but it remained the ideal. The task here is not to define or delimit roles but to indicate that there is strong evidence that gender was not a major consideration concerning leadership in these churches. Men and women assumed leadership roles and Paul and the author of Acts take that for granted.

The roles women play in the canonical gospels carry the limitations found in the study of forms, sources, the *Sitz im Leben* of a particular pericope or section, literary and historical elements, redactional principles. Granting these limitations, it can be pointed out that women are chief characters in at least twenty-one incidents where they are named in the four canonical gospels. They appear as chief characters in thirty-one other incidents where they are not named. Luke pairs stories of men and women. In the fourth gospel a woman is the first to proclaim the risen Jesus to the disciples (John 20:1–18); a woman was the first to spread the news of Jesus' presence (John 4:28–30) and a woman was the first to proclaim him Messiah (John 11:27). It is possible to wonder if the unnamed companion of Cleopas on the road to Emmaus might have been a woman, since the names of women are so frequently omitted. In addition, there is ample evidence that the word, "disciple," as used in the canonical gospels, is gender-inclusive. Luke describes three women who were with Jesus, who were disciples and who provided for Jesus and the others from their means.

There are many unanswered questions about the roles of women in the time of Jesus and in the time of the writing of the gospels. Their presence is unmistakable but often obscured by the processes of transmission. Stories that belie any attempt to limit discipleship to men were so strong in the tradition that they are found in all three synoptic gospels: the cure of Peter's mother-in-law; Jesus' unsettling relationship with his own mother and brothers; the conflated stories of Jairus's daughter and the woman with a hemorrhage; Herodias; the woman who anointed Jesus' feet in the house at Bethany; the young girls in the courtyard who terrorize Peter, and the women who bear news of resurrection. Women populate the gospels and epistles as clearly as men do.

Mary of Magdala was strikingly prominent in the apocryphal gospels. She assumes a role of leadership there. The picture of women in the canonical writings helps to verify that women did enjoy such places in the early church and that Mary of Magdala could have been prominent among them.

CHAPTER 8

Conclusions

This study began with questions: Who was Mary of Magdala? What role did she play in the life of the early Christian communities? Was it possible and even probable that Mary of Magdala was an apostle and an important leader in the early church? The method has been to employ some of the results of historical criticism combined with literary criticism in order to come to an understanding of the social, economic and political background, the use of terms chosen to describe those who followed Jesus in the New Testament texts, and then to examine the actual wording of the narratives, canonical and apocryphal, in which Mary of Magdala appears. It has not been a conscious effort to produce a "feminist study," important as such efforts are, even though that may seem to be the direction of the work. The task was to read the texts as they were written and to attempt to understand them as the texts themselves would indicate particular understandings. Rigorous attention to the texts results in the conclusion that, without doubt, Mary of Magdala was acknowledged as an apostle in the early Christian church and that she was a leader of considerable influence even rivaling Peter.

Once the associations of Mary of Magdala with the "sinful woman" portrayal had been eliminated, and they should have been eliminated almost without comment, it was necessary to disengage her from among the other Marys in the canonical texts—Mary, the mother of Jesus, Mary of Bethany and the "other Mary." It was necessary to clarify these distinctions before the actual study of the texts and the milieu could begin.

It was also necessary to examine the canonical gospels carefully to try to determine if there is evidence that Mary of Magdala was, indeed, apostle and leader in the early church. One counter-argument to the fact that Mary was important is the omission of her name from Paul's list of those who had experienced appearances of the risen Lord, the list found in First Corinthians, chapter 15. There are several fairly easy ways to explain this omission. Paul was writing kerygma, not appearance narratives. There are many other discrepancies between Paul's list and the recipients of appearances in the canonical gospels, and usually buried under this accusation that Paul omitted Mary's name deliberately is the unsustainable accusation that Paul was a misogynist. The kerygma of First Corinthians 15 cannot be used to discredit the important role played by Mary of Magdala.

There is also suspicion that the terms "the Twelve," "disciple" and "apostle," which today we try to make very clear and precise, were not so to the gospel writers, and it is necessary to understand that they did not use them in a clear and precise manner. So the modern tendency to consider "disciple" as an exclusively male designation is erroneous, or at least inaccurate. The gospel writers can write "twelve disciples" in one sentence and refer to the "twelve apostles" in the next (Matt 10:1–5); and "those present along with the Twelve" (Mark 4:10). Or "when day came, he called his disciples to himself, and from them he chose Twelve, who he also named apostles" (Luke 6:13). These, and many other uses of the terms indicate a very fluid understanding of the composition of the groups. By the time of the writing of the gospels clear distinctions were obfuscated by interchangeable designations. This fluidity makes it easy to see that women were included in the bands of disciples following Jesus. Luke does this in 8:1–3. They were thought of and spoken of in the same way as the male disciples and their personal allegiance to Jesus was based upon devotion and intensity, not upon gender.

The conclusion, then, is clear. Mary of Magdala was most certainly a disciple of Jesus, one of a group of female disciples who were women of rank and means mentioned in all three synoptic gospels. She was an apostle in the absolute sense that Paul uses in defining his own apostleship. The apostle is one who has seen the Lord. It should also be noted that Paul is not "apostle to the Corinthians" because he reports to the Corinthians of his having seen the Lord, nor is Mary of Magdala simply apostle to the disciples because she reports the resurrection to them. Nor is there any evidence at all for attempting to limit Mary's apostleship to a mission for women only. There is no evidence of this in any of the documents, and evidence to the contrary is found in most of them. These two misinterpretations are later explanations placed on texts that intend no such distinctions.

A significant piece of evidence that Mary of Magdala was an important leader in the early church can be found in the grammatical form by which she is consistently described. The consistency of the use of this form provides strong evidence that it had become common usage, that Mary had become well known and that her name had become almost a title, not unlike "Jesus of Nazareth," or "Mary of Scotland," or "Ignatius of Loyola." These are less attempts to identify someone by a geographical reference than they are names which have become technical: they identify this person because most people know to whom the words apply.

In addition to its importance as an indicator of Mary's place among the people of the early church, there is significance in the fact that Mary's name survived the redactions of the early ages of the written documents. The names of other women were omitted from final redactions, the Samaritan woman at the well being one notable example. The fact that the name of Mary of Magdala survived the initial reluctance to use women's names and the redactional process, by which some names were eliminated, indicates that she was too well known in the early church for her name to have been suppressed in any way. She was part of an oral tradition too well attested to admit of change. It is, in any case, strong evidence that she had importance and authority.

The Synoptic Gospels

The portrayal of Mary of Magdala in the synoptic gospels places her definitively in the role of leader, faithful disciple, courageous provider and messenger of resurrection. The synoptic accounts follow a basic narrative and the place of Mary of Magdala is one element of this basic narrative. She is the leader of the deed and she is one of the unifying elements among the stories of crucifixion, burial and empty-tomb events. The consistent use of her name, always first on the list, unlike the mixing of the names of the other women, adds still more recognition of this woman's primary role. The irony of the faithful presence of the women and the desertion by the male disciples is stressed in Mark and continued in both Matthew and Luke. It also dramatizes the difference between the cowardice of Peter and the stalwart courage of Mary and her companions. The presence of a fairly large group of women disciples at the crucifixion scene should be noted because it provides the only relief, slight though it be, from the forsakenness that Mark portrays so well in the crucifixion account. The theme of abandonment is employed by Matthew and Luke but with less intensity. The use of such a humiliating theme causes suspicion that a historical reality underlies the story.

In the four canonical gospels, while four different reasons for the early morning journey to the tomb are given, they are clearly based on one basic tradition. The slight variations indicate that the tradition about their going out was very strong but that the community behind each gospel did not agree about the details of the story. The confusion about the rolling away of the stone stems from the same reality as does the variation in description of the heavenly messengers—one man, two men, one angel, two angels. In such a manner it can be seen that there existed a strong oral tradition which included the day and hour of the visit, concern about the stone, a message delivered by heavenly messengers, and the presence of Mary of Magdala. These were *sine qua non* elements of the first narratives of resurrection. Differing details in the narrative fit the redactional concerns of the individual accounts—for example, Matthew's inclusion of apocalyptic signs fits his concern with the Hebrew scriptures' portrayals of manifestations of God's power.

In Matthew's empty-tomb narrative, there is difficulty over the singular verb that occurs in the first verse of chapter 28. The verb "she came" is clearly singular and contributes to the sense that in the original tradition Mary of Magdala went alone to the empty tomb on Easter morning. The "other Mary" seems to have been added on, and later other women's names were added. Since Mary of Magdala's role, in any case, was clearly to be the leader, to be concerned about finding Jesus' body, and to hear and relay the message of the heavenly envoys, the other women became less than essential. Quite possibly their names were added to give more substance to the witness. Mary was the one who cared, who performed acts of devotion, who was deemed worthy to carry the all-important message.

The Lukan narrative gives added attention to women at the same time that it subsumes some of Mary of Magdala's leadership role into the category of "the women." The list in chapter 8 includes women who were wealthy, independent, and of high social and political standing. Mary of Magdala stands at the head of the list.

These women are described as disciples and deacons who ministered to the needs of the other disciples. The description depicts a genuine community of disciples and its composition of men and women is passed over without comment. It would seem that no comment is required: that reality was simply the way it was.

In the crucifixion scene in Luke, Jesus' acquaintances, again with no gender distinction, are standing at a distance. But only the women, those mentioned in chapter 8, go to see where he is laid, and only the women go to the tomb and receive the message of resurrection. Mary of Magdala is listed first, but the concern of this redactor seems to be to place women in these three key incidents. The Lukan redactor makes explicit what is only hinted at in Mark and Matthew: that the "apostles," to whom the women relate the story, do not believe it. This, too, stresses the contrast between the women disciples who believe and male disciples who do not. The overall effect of these portrayals is to emphasize the role played by women in the ministry of Jesus especially in the final scenes of that ministry.

The Fourth Gospel

In the fourth gospel, women are very important. Jesus' mother at the wedding at Cana, the Samaritan woman at the well, Martha and Mary, Mary the wife of Clopas and Mary of Magdala all have highly significant roles. Three of them—the Samaritan woman, Martha and Mary of Magdala—are primary proclaimers of Jesus in this gospel. And in John 11:27, Martha even plays the role awarded to Peter in the synoptics (Mark 8:29, Matt 16:16 and Luke 9:20).

The general atmosphere of the fourth gospel is such that the important roles given to these women fit the narrative pattern. The description of Jesus' death, for example, while depicting it in a kingly manner, also depicts a personal and intimate scene. Those present include Jesus' mother and her sister, Mary of Magdala and, even though he is not listed among those present, the "beloved disciple" clearly is also there. Jesus' mother and her sister are present by right of relationship, and the "beloved disciple" is there to assume care of Mary. Mary of Magdala has no such reason to be included. She is not there because of relationship as the other two women are, nor by reason of a mission to be assigned to her, as the "beloved disciple" is. She is there because she had an established place in the crucifixion account and because that place could not be ignored. Once again, her importance is obvious.

Cogent reasons have been cited for positing that the accounts of the "race narrative" between Peter and the "other disciple" and the appearance of Jesus to Mary of Magdala are parallel episodes in the empty-tomb narrative of the fourth gospel. The structure of John 20:1–18 indicates a parallel. The race pericope and the appearance to Mary of Magdala demonstrate a parallel; the use of Johannine devices indicates it and the contrast between the faith of Mary and the questionable reaction of the disciples indicates it. The two disciples witnessed the empty tomb and went away: Mary of Magdala witnessed the empty tomb, searched and found and then went to the other disciples (presumably Peter and the "other disciple" among them) and reported that she had seen the Lord. The story of the two disciples is detached, unemotional and objective. The story of the appearance to Mary of Magdala has a sense of intimacy and personal encounter that makes it subjective and emotional.

In the appearance story (John 20:14–18), Mary of Magdala is characterized with precision and care. She is an example of total devotion both in going out to the tomb and in her anxiety to anoint the body of Jesus. The threefold repetition of her question about the whereabouts of the body which she believed to have been stolen denotes a single-minded devotion to the Jesus she knew and loved and who had died and been buried. The text portrays her as totally without suspicion of resurrection. The theme of her concern to recover the body of Jesus is continued by the use of the verb, "turned." Mary turned away from the tomb and all that it implied. She turned herself to the person she believed to be the gardener. Only after Jesus had called her by name did she turn again, and, in a moment, accept the fact of resurrection. Then she was sent to the disciples to tell them that she had seen the Lord. There can be no room to doubt the importance of Mary's role in the fourth gospel's empty-tomb narrative. She was the devoted follower who came to the tomb without any inkling of a supernatural intervention on Jesus' behalf. She was doing the service that a devout follower might be expected to do. She reacted the same way. She informed the disciples of the empty tomb but continued to weep and search for the body she believed to have been stolen. Only the call by Jesus himself allowed her to realize what had occurred. With the same kind of devotion and enthusiasm she went to announce the fact of resurrection to the disciples. Here, too, there can be no doubt about the importance of Mary of Magdala.

There always remains the question of the actual situation that lay behind the gospel texts, the *Sitz im Leben,* and therein lies the answer to the questions proposed at the beginning of this study. If Mary of Magdala's name remained in the texts even to the point of dramatizing the absence of male disciples, and if her name is consistently used in a form that had become technical by the time of the writing of the gospels, it becomes obvious that her influence and her story were treasured in the early church. Even more, it indicates that the name of Mary of Magdala was inextricably united with the developing realization of the reality of resurrection and that her place in the narratives that dramatized it was necessary.

Women in the Ancient World

The place women occupied in the ancient world provided one clue to the possibility that Mary of Magdala was a person of some stature in the early Christian community. Roman law was largely unequivocal about the role of women—they were to remain subject to men and were regarded, legally, as the property of men. However, the ambiguities, interpretations, misinterpretations and circumventions of Roman laws in general and laws regarding women in particular were so blatant that a real gap could be seen to have existed between the law itself and the accepted practices of the time.

Epigraphic and inscriptional evidence contradicts, in part, the picture provided by the study of Roman law and even of much Roman history. Women fulfilled important roles in political, social and religious circles in Rome itself and in the rest of the Empire. Some women earned high ranks as officials in their governments. There are multiple examples of such leadership roles for women and their combined force is to leave no doubt about the fact that some women broke out of the legal restraints of the time and some men evidently allowed them to do so. This is not to deny that women were oppressed and dominated in the ancient world but indicates that there can be no valid monolithic picture of women in the ancient world, as has been assumed until recently. There is much evidence that then, as now, some oppressed individuals were able to find their way out of that oppression and some of the oppressors were wise enough to allow this escape, even to encourage it. Thus, it is not at all impossible that Mary of Magdala could have risen to a high position in the early church as other women surely had done at that time.

The Apocrypha

Beyond the possibility that Mary of Magdala could have been an important leader in the early church lies the question of its probability. Is there reason to believe that Mary of Magdala could have been a leader in the early church? The evidence from the canonical gospels certainly supports that contention. The evidence of the apocryphal gospels is even stronger that Mary was, indeed, very prominent, that she was respected and treated with deference, that she was an acknowledged leader. Lest anyone write this off as a figment of the imagination of those "gnostic women writers" who made a heroine of Mary, it is important to note that not all of the apocryphal literature can be classified as gnostic, and it cannot be proven that women wrote all or any part of that literature. Some of the apocryphal literature is clearly anti-gnostic. Other writings of the time contain gnostic elements but are not specifically, nor completely, gnostic in orientation. The gnostic writings themselves need not be eliminated simply because there is suspicion that they were written by women. Nevertheless, it is important to bear in mind that they were pronounced heretical by the church authorities of that day. The accumulated evidence makes it impossible to ignore the effect of the references to Mary of Magdala just as the accumulated effect of the inscriptional evidence made it impossible to ignore the important roles some women played in the ancient world.

The *Epistula Apostolorum* and "The Gospel of Peter" are two significant apocryphal writings that feature Mary of Magdala as the leader of the women who go to the empty tomb and as the chosen messenger to other disciples. The two roles are clearly delineated in both: she is the leader who brings the other women to the tomb, and she is sent to announce the news of resurrection to the other disciples.

An important aspect of the apocryphal writings that occurs with startling consistency is the description of Mary of Magdala in conflict with Peter. The disagreement seems always to begin with Peter who cannot feature that the Lord would reveal himself first to a woman. "The Gospel of Thomas" clearly places Mary in a position equal to that of Peter. Another writing, "The Dialog of the Savior," deals with sexuality as the dividing line between those who are acceptable and those who are not. The polemic with Peter continues in many of the noncanonical writings and culminates in the "Gospel of Mary" where Levi pronounces that the Lord loved Mary more than he loved his male disciples. It is difficult, if not dangerous, to read these gospels with too literal an interpretation but the continuing presence of conflict between Peter and Mary of Magdala is pervasive and gives rise at least to the suspicion that there was such a conflict in the early churches and the devotees of Mary of Magdala may well have been in serious conflict with the devotees of Peter.

There are many references to women active in the Pauline churches. Paul lists "coworkers," "deacons," "apostles" and heads of house churches. It is impossible to read the authentic Pauline literature without recognizing that many women were important to Paul and to the churches he shepherded.

The word "disciple" in the canonical gospels is used as gender-inclusive. This is in addition to the fact that many women are mentioned in these texts. The use of the word "disciple" to indicate only males would seem to have developed later in the church, perhaps at the time that Mary of Magdala was being assigned the role of harlot. Women play important roles in the gospels: they minister to Jesus and to his disciples; they come to seek healing for themselves and for their loved ones; they are the subject matter of parables and teachings; they are present in the sorrowful last days when real courage was required to remain with Jesus.

It might be assumed that a sizable segment of the early church population was responsible for keeping the name of Mary of Magdala in the texts and for continuing the description of prominence that she had held since the time of Jesus. It is impossible, of course, to reconstruct the historical situation of any part of

Palestine in the time between the death of Jesus and the time of the writing of the canonical gospels. We are almost totally without documents from that time and have no reliable information at all about what was transpiring in Galilee, let alone in the town of Magdala. Since, however, the canonical gospels were written away from Galilee and significantly later than the events therein described, it is impossible to deny that the traditions about Mary of Magdala were firmly entrenched and widespread. To have found their way into all four gospels with increasing rather than decreasing importance is remarkable. To have maintained the one form of identification is equally remarkable in an age when names were frequently mixed. To have been the only person, male or female, listed in all four gospels as the first to realize that Jesus had risen and to have announced that message to the other disciples was to have reached undeniable prominence. In the early church there has to have been a strong tradition built upon more than pious interpretations, a tradition that almost certainly rested on some historical reality. Early church tradition awards Mary of Magdala the following titles: Apostle because she had seen the Lord; disciple because she had followed the Lord; deacon because she had ministered to him and to his other disciples; evangelizer because she was sent out with the message that Jesus Christ had risen; and leader because the written evidence portrays her thus. The irrefutable fact is that the name of Mary of Magdala is essentially bound up with the central Christian reality—humankind's realization that resurrection had occurred.

Mary of Magdala Today

How has it come to pass that an intriguing mystery story became a best-selling novel while raising many questions about Mary of Magdala? In recent years scholars have written excellent studies about Mary of Magdala, one of the best of which is Susan Haskins' *Mary Magdalene: Myth and Metaphor.* Unfortunately, the mystery story has reached a large number of readers; the scholarship has not. Dan Brown, in *The Da Vinci Code,* claims to have written a novel—and to give the book its due, it is a good novel, a gripping mystery story and an overall "good read." The author has fictionalized many parts of the story and embellished others. He creates a difficulty by prefacing the work with a claim that large parts of the story are historically accurate. This dual purpose results in serious misdirection—most often through exaggeration, distortion and outright fictionalizing of details that are presented as historical.

Brown's treatment of Constantine furnishes a good example. Indeed, Constantine played a significant part in the radical change that took place in the early fourth century. Many factors entered into that change that had begun before Constantine and continued after his death. Even though Brown portrays Constantine as the villain who brought about all the changes, he is correct in pointing out that, in this period of history, the role of women was totally reversed from what it had been before his time. From the beginning of Christianity, women had played important roles in Church life.

In the fourth century, a variety of factors led to the reversal of this situation. Brown portrays this, but with generalizations rather than facts. Brown would have served his readers much better if he had made clear that this trend was historically verifiable and that his tracing of Sophie's lineage was pure fiction.

A serious distortion occurs in *The Da Vinci Code in* the morphing of the Holy Grail into a person who was fathered by Jesus. This is wildly imaginative and somewhat disrespectful, not because many people believe that Jesus never married, but because it shifts the focus from Mary of Magdala, apostle and leader, to Mary of Magdala, wife and mother. This is sheer fiction. Also in this book, the pictures of the fanatic Silas and of the Opus Dei leader Bishop Aringarosa help to support a suspicion that there is more than a little bit of anti-Catholicism in the portrayals. This curious amalgam of fact and fiction does a disservice to history and to the Church and even to its detractors. Brown's contention that the figure seated next to Jesus in Da Vinci's painting of the Last Supper is a woman requires several baseless assumptions. And then to ask the reader to believe that that person was Mary of Magdala is a serious stretch.

The purpose of this study has been to portray Mary of Magdala as she is pictured in the canonical and noncanonical writings and to examine the grievous wrong that corrupted her image through the ages. Mary of Magdala offers an important example of good leadership for the Church today. She also defines a spirituality that can be both gender-inclusive and specifically feminine.

Christians today do well to study Mary of Magdala as a leader whose total devotion and self-assurance enabled her to act upon her own convictions without concern about opposition, hostility or improbability. She provided the example of an individual who stood tall for what she believed and for the Lord whom she loved. She is portrayed as a woman who could demonstrate loving devotion without concern for her own position or for what anyone else might think. It is possible that the evolution of this early church leader into harlot, and then into penitent sinner, reflects the discomfort some later writers felt in acknowledging the true nature of the picture given of Mary of Magdala in the canonical and apocryphal literatures.

It is impossible to deny Mary of Magdala's leadership role. She is depicted in this role in every mention of her in the canonical and apocryphal writings. No explanations or reasons for her leadership are given; it is simply accepted. This leads to the conclusion that the texts allow her to be portrayed as a leader because she was, in fact, a leader. The gospel portrait seems to reflect a well-recognized leader. There do not seem to have been any insurmountable obstacles in her way. There is no hint of displeasure with her leadership. Perhaps through the force of her personality, perhaps because of the circumstances of Jesus' itinerant preaching, perhaps because of the general makeup of the band of disciples who followed Jesus, there appears to have been total ease in the early Christian church with the portrayal of Mary of Magdala as a key player in the drama. It is no small matter that she is portrayed as standing by the cross, witnessing the burial, discovering the empty tomb, recording the first appearance of the risen Christ. Her name is always mentioned first in the group of women. In her world, the order of naming indicated the order of importance.

The account of Jesus' appearance to Mary of Magdala in the fourth gospel sheds light on her relationship with Jesus, on her position in the church and on her continued influence in the postapostolic church. The tradition of her leadership was, evidently, of importance. For this or for some other reason, the portrayal of Mary of Magdala as leader arouses no suspicion, no hostility, no opposition, at least as it is presented in the canonical texts. This might well indicate that there was a gender-inclusive time when the word "disciple" meant all followers of Jesus, all members of the body of Christ, all who were "learners." Women were accepted into that group with no distinctions made. None seemed necessary.

Leadership

To discern the pattern of leadership manifested by Mary of Magdala it is relevant to examine how she acquired such a position. From the texts it appears that Mary was the kind of person who automatically acquired followers. Her role is taken for granted when she leads those who support and minister to Jesus (Luke 8:1–3), and when she leads the group of women to the scene of the crucifixion. It is easy to see from these portrayals that Mary was, first of all, a fervently devoted follower of Jesus. Evidently no obstacle was too great to be overcome, no custom too important to impede an action she felt to be important, no action of other disciples so disconcerting as to limit her courage. Her presence at the crucifixion, burial and empty tomb bespeaks the kind of courage that inspires others. It had required great courage and substantial devotion to defy custom and to travel with Jesus and his other disciples. Although no comment is made on this in the gospel accounts, it must have been unusual, possibly even provocative. Given the financial limitations the Empire attempted to impose on women, it required expertise and courage to expend funds on Jesus' enterprise. Mary's appeal to the alleged gardener in the fourth gospel account is done without hesitation. Her only concern is to find the dead body of Jesus: she is neither fearful nor hesitant. The writers portray all this without any hint of opposition or even of wonderment. This is the way that Mary of Magdala was perceived in the early church. She was a woman who followed Jesus single-mindedly. She led others to the same kind of commitment and she demonstrated whatever courage and ingenuity were required for what was all-embracing for her. Her leadership was a natural outcome of her intense feeling and devotion.

Another aspect of the picture of Mary of Magdala in the canonical gospels that contributes to a portrait of real leadership is her self-control and patience. She is willing to sit outside the tomb and wait—it would seem that she had no clue as to what she was awaiting. She waits out the Sabbath rest and comes to the empty tomb early on the third day. She runs to Peter and to the other disciple and waits for them to leave before she begins her own search. She is not attempting to force an issue, to hurry developments, to supersede any other person or persons. Quietly, and without attracting any attention from guards or disciples, she single-mindedly pursues the quest for the dead body of Jesus. She is not deterred from her task even by the person she assumes to be the gardener. Her only interest in him is to find out if he knows where the body of Jesus has been taken. It is impossible to attribute to Mary of Magdala any motive of curiosity or self-aggrandizement. Her motive is purely devotion to the Lord she loves and believes she has lost.

The important mission Jesus gave to Mary of Magdala when he sent her to proclaim resurrection to his disciples strengthens belief in her leadership role. Jesus makes Mary understand that she can no longer look upon him as the person she knew and loved. She is the person to whom he says that he has not yet ascended and become the risen Christ. The concept of ascension is mentioned here for one of only two references in the gospels. In the Lukan narrative, the ascension is clearly closure: Jesus is taken up into heaven and his mission passes to the disciples. In the fourth gospel account Mary alone is given to understand this new reality and she is sent to relay the knowledge to others. The inclusiveness of "my Father and your Father, my God and your God" (John 20:17) renders this message, and the communication of it, of supreme importance. Mary announces to the brethren both resurrection and ascension—the continuity of the risen and ascended Christ with the Jesus they had known on earth. In Luke, Jesus explains himself and acts. In the fourth gospel, Mary of Magdala is the one who acts. No one questioned her right to act and surely no one questioned Jesus' right to send her. She is unquestionably cast as primary messenger of the great mystery of salvation.

What does all this say to the woman of the twenty-first century about women's leadership in the Church today? Few women today are in the position where they can simply be the leaders they are, without arousing suspicion, opposition, hostility—often all three. Mary must have been conscious of some undercurrents of dissatisfaction with her roles from the men around her. The apocryphal literature develops this theme often and at length. The important factor, it seems, for inspiring feminine leadership today is the fact that Mary did not fight, she did not argue, she did not threaten. She simply led. She went her way and did what she considered appropriate according to the understanding of her position that she had learned from Jesus. She was who she was and she worried about it not at all. Probably some of her fortitude came from being able to ignore innuendos, opposition, threats from any who challenged her leadership. She seems not to have experienced, or at least not to have reacted to, opposition. Mary of Magdala was her own person, she acted according to her own beliefs and loves: she did not become involved in fighting her way to these roles. Mary demonstrates mature self-confidence to perfection. The gospel portrait of Mary of Magdala provides an inspiring paradigm for true leadership that is not gender-dependent.

Devotion

It would be unwise to attempt to separate Mary's spirituality from her leadership role but for purposes of study, it is helpful. She provides a leadership model for modern women in their quest for feminine spirituality. Mary's presence at the three final scenes of Jesus' life—the crucifixion, burial and empty tomb—manifests the courage and leadership that result from devotion and love. The male followers seem not yet possessed of such all-powerful devotion: they are controlled by fear until after the appearance of the risen Christ. Mary and her women companions are controlled by devotion from their first appearance in the gospel.

The intensity and intimacy of Mary's devotion is manifested tellingly in the fourth gospel account of the events at the empty tomb. The historicity of the account is not at issue here; the portrayal by the early church is. Mary is selflessly searching for the body of Jesus.

She has no hint of an understanding of resurrection—she searches exclusively for a dead body. At a key moment in the narrative Mary is able to "turn herself around," and by that action opens herself to the possibility that her quest may not be as important as she thinks it is. The verb "turn around" is used twice in the garden scene and it provides the key to the intensity of feeling and devotion that Mary manifested. She turned away from the quest for the dead body and then she turned herself toward the Lord who had called her by name. The verb indicates positive action on her part and her turning has to do with Jesus, not with herself. She is able to turn from the totally human act of attempting to give adequate burial to a dead body, to belief in resurrection, in the mystery of God's saving love in a form she had not even considered until that moment. Her belief is so complete and so strong that she can become the proclaimer of that news to the other disciples. She is also called upon to proclaim the ascension of Jesus. In the fourth gospel, the ascension reference affirms the inclusion of all Jesus' disciples in his glory, "My Father and your Father, my God and your God" (John 20:17).

The type of devotion Mary manifests here is eminently worthy of imitation. Mary believes fervently in Jesus even before she understands completely who he is and what his life and death mean. The intensity of her feeling, which manifests itself in each of the scenes, forms her devotion. What she knows is important: what she feels is even more crucial. It is obvious that her devotion is not dependent upon the people around her or on those around Jesus. Her concern about human reactions seems to have been nil since it is never mentioned. Her devotion is to the person of Jesus and in that she is single-minded. This spirituality is distinctly feminine but not gender-exclusive.

The development of the story of Mary of Magdala from apostle and leader to harlot and then to repentant sinner was traced in the Introduction. In spite of the inaccuracy of that portrait, the misinterpretation exists and can be instructive. It reflects a common experience of women today. Many women live through opposition and hostility when they attempt to move beyond the traditional roles permitted to women in this society. Mary of Magdala's role was changed from an intensely positive one to an equally negative one. With that, many women can identify. Their efforts can be misconstrued by ascribing unworthy motives to them, by misrepresentation, by outright dishonesty. Through the centuries the story of Mary of Magdala has undergone radical diminution and the present-day revival of her true story should serve, perhaps, as a source of hope that women will be able to achieve their rightful place. A woman who manifested self-confidence, mature leadership, intense devotion and total competence became, at the hands of some men, a prostitute, a symbol of sin, a degraded human being whose chief claim to remembrance was her intense sorrow for sin and her extreme efforts to redeem herself from that sin. She can surely serve today as a model for those women who suffer similar indignities.

Mary of Magdala and Mary, the Mother of Jesus

Through the ages there has been an unusual relationship between devotion to Mary of Magdala and devotion to Mary, the mother of Jesus. It has been mentioned that some critics have been embarrassed by the fact that Mary of Magdala is consistently pictured at the scenes of the end of Jesus' life whereas Jesus' mother's presence is only mentioned at the crucifixion account in the fourth gospel. There is no recorded appearance of the risen Christ to his mother, while there is recorded an intensely personal encounter between Jesus and Mary of Magdala both in the fourth gospel and in Matthew's account.

Perhaps one of the keys to this enigma can be found in the fact that the gospel portrait of Mary, the mother of Jesus, needs to be read as it is, not as legend and devotion have romanticized it. According to the canonical gospels, Mary's pregnancy was suspect—both Matthew and Luke work to offset this accusation. Her son left her, according to several accounts; he placed his followers before her (Mark 3:31–35 and parallels). Mary lived, according to the fourth gospel, to see her son executed as a convicted felon. This real portrait is, at best, grim; it was rapidly superseded by romantic legends. As a result, the real portrait of the mother of Jesus receded and the romanticized version became popular. The romanticized version is much less human than the real one. Eventually, romantic legend placed the mother of Jesus in a transcendent position where her humanity was obscured.

The story of Mary of Magdala somehow offsets the distorted picture of Mary, the mother of Jesus. Mary of Magdala—heroically standing by the cross, leading a group of women, searching for the body of Jesus—has all the terribly human characteristics that the portrait of the mother of Jesus had but of which it has been robbed by romantic legend. This helps to make understandable the ease by which Mary of Magdala became the repentant sinner—an all too human reality. The humanness of Mary of Magdala made of her an object of devotion, whereas the semidivinizing of the mother of Jesus removed her from the realm of the attainable.

It can be said that Mary of Magdala is an exemplar par excellence of devotion and intensity of feeling for the historical Jesus and for faithful continuance of feeling and devotion for the risen Christ. Mary personifies deep devotion, proper employment of feeling, courage, openness, readiness to change radically when called upon to do so. She can serve as a role model for the mature, self-confident woman who is content to be herself. Mary did not look for or notice opposition or hostility, and apparently was victim of very little of it during her lifetime. She led a group of women, and there is no evidence that anyone had any difficulty with that. Mary of Magdala's spirituality was built upon the solid rocks of realistic self-esteem, deep love for God, devotion to those around her, love for her community and intense devotion to the person of Jesus. There can be no better foundation.

Conclusion

For women of today, Mary most certainly provides a model of leadership. Women in our society who wait for men to yield places of leadership to them usually wait a long time. Women who recognize their own gifts and have the self-confidence to be who they are and to do what they do best, lead when leadership is called for. If hostility, opposition, suspicion occur, true leaders are not deterred.

Leadership is often woman's gift from the Spirit of God, she who inspires all leadership.

In addition to this role model as leader, the gospel portrait of Mary of Magdala portrays her as disciple in the truest meaning of that word. Mary and her companions were followers of Jesus who were learning (the Greek word for disciple means "one who is learning"). They rendered diaconal service, "they ministered to him" (Mark 15:41, Matt 27:55, Luke 8:1–3). Mary was commissioned by Jesus to be an evangelizer, to "tell my brothers to go to Galilee, and there they will see me" (Matt 28:10). She was sent to the disciples where she assumed the role of apostle: "I have seen the Lord" (John 20:18). This gospel portrait depicts the fullness of women's roles in the church—they are called to discipleship, to diaconal service, to evangelization and to apostleship.

Men and women of today might look to Mary of Magdala as inspiration for devotion. Few people deny woman's ability to be thoroughly committed to other people, to causes and to beliefs. Mary exemplifies this type of commitment. The intensity of feeling that she demonstrates is a characteristic that women may well be encouraged to emulate. Intensity of feeling, self-control, willingness to sacrifice to a reality she recognized to be beyond her human understanding—all these characteristics make Mary of Magdala an apt model for the spirituality of all people today.

Mary of Magdala was a woman, and as a woman she provides inspiration to other women today. Above all, she personifies a willingness to pursue the ideal as she saw it, without regard to those who might try to dissuade her. She could be who she was. This gospel picture calls to women of today to be who they truly are.

Notes

Introduction

1. Dan Brown, *The Da Vinci Code* (New York: Doubleday, 2003), 442.

2. Marjorie Malvern, *Venus in Sackcloth* (Carbondale: South Illinois University Press, 1975), 69.

3. Brown, *The Da Vinci Code,* 124.

4. Marina Warner, *Alone of All Her Sex* (New York: Vintage, 1976), 228.

5. Charles C. Merow, *The Letters of Saint Jerome* (New York: Newman, 1963), 157.

6. Raymond-Leopold Bruckberger, *Mary Magdalene* (New York: Pantheon, 1953), 228.

7. Montague Rhodes James, *The Apocryphal New Testament* (Oxford: Oxford University Press, 1924), 87.

8. Jonathan Sumption, *Pilgrimage: An Image of Medieval Religion* (Totowa, NJ: Rowman and Littlefield, 1975), 36.

9. Jacobus de Voragine, *The Golden Legend,* vol. 2 (New York: Longmans, 1941), 362.

10. Sumption, *Pilgrimage,* 36.

11. de Voragine, *The Golden Legend,* 355.

12. Ibid., 356.

13. Ibid., 357.

14. Rosalind and Christopher Brooke, *Popular Religion in the Middle Ages* (London: Thames and Hudson, 1984), 92.

15. Victor Saxer, *Le Culte de Marie Madeleine en Occident, dès Origines à la fin du Moyen-Âge.* 2 vols. (Paris: Librarie Clavreuil, 1959), "Cartes" following p. 182.

Chapter 1. Related Questions

1. Excerpts from *The Gospel of Thomas,* in Willis Barnstone, ed., *The Other Bible* (San Francisco: Harper & Row, 1984), 307.

2 Brown, *The Da Vinci Code,* 442.

3. Excerpts from *The Gospel of Philip,* in James M. Robinson, ed., *The Nag Hammadi Library,* rev. ed. (San Francisco: HarperCollins, 1990), 135.

4. Ibid., 63:34-35.

5. Norval Geldenhuys, *Commentary on the Gospel of Luke* (Grand Rapids: Eerdmans, 1968), 239.

6. Jane Schaberg, "How Mary Magdalene Became a Whore." *Bible Review* 8:5 (1992), 30-37.

7. George A. Buttrick, *Interpreter's Dictionary of the Bible* (Nashville: Abingdon, 1962), 288.

8. Ephraim the Syrian, "Homily on Our Lord," no. 47, in Philip Schaff and Henry Wace, eds., *Nicene and Post-Nicene Fathers of the Christian Church,* vol. 13 (Grand Rapids: Eerdmans, 1983), 326–327.

9. Gregory the Great, "Homilarum Evangelii," in Jacques-Paul Migne, *Patrologiae Latina,* vol. 76, 2.23.76. The translation is the author's own.

10. David Mycoff, trans. and ed., *The Life of Saint Mary Magdalene and of Her Sister Saint Martha: A Medieval Biography* (Kalamazoo: Cistercian Publications, 1989).

11. Carole Straw, *Gregory the Great* (Berkeley: Berkeley University Press, 1988), 139.

Chapter 2. Scriptural Evidence

1. Reginald H. Fuller, *The Formation of the Resurrection Narratives* (New York: Macmillan, 1971), 28.

2. Ibid., 29.

3. Edward Lynn Bode, *The First Easter Morning* (Rome: Biblical Institute Press, 1970), 91.

4. Fuller, *Resurrection Narratives,* 27–30.

5. Herman Ridderbos, *Paul: An Outline of His Theology* (Grand Rapids: Eerdmans, 1975), 199.

6. Fuller, *Resurrection Narratives,* 27–30.

7. E. P. Sanders, *Jesus and Judaism* (London: SCM, 1985), 106.

8. David Noel Freedman, ed., *The Anchor Bible Dictionary,* vol. 2 (New York: Doubleday, 1992), 206.

9. Ibid., 208.

10. Freedman, *Anchor Bible Dictionary,* vol. 6, 601–602.

11. Rivka Gauer, *Biblical Holy Places: An Illustrated Guide* (London: A.E. Black Ltd., 1987), 185.

12. Paul L. Maier, *Josephus: The Essential Writings* (Grand Rapids: Kregal Publications, 1988), 309–311.

13. Gauer, *Biblical Holy Places,* 184.

14. Michael Avi-Yonah, *The Holy Land* (London: Thames and Hudson, 1972), 73.

15. Ibid., 79.

16. James H. Moulton, *Grammar of New Testament Greek* (Edinburgh: T and T Clark, 1922), 171.

17. Friedrich William Blass and Albert De Brunner, *A Greek Grammar of the New Testament* (Chicago: University of Chicago Press, 1962), 136.

18. Ibid., 136.

19. Moulton, *Grammar of New Testament Greek,* 206.

20. Bruce M. Metzger, *A Textual Commentary on the Greek New Testament* (London: United Bible Societies, 1971), 184.

21. Blass and De Brunner, *Greek Grammar,* 30.

Chapter 3. Mary of Magdala in Mark and Matthew

1. Reginald Fuller, *The Formation of the Resurrection Narratives* (New York: Macmillan, 1971), 52.

2. John E. Alsup, *The Post-Resurrection Appearance Stories of the Gospel Tradition: A History-of-Tradition Analysis with Text Synopsis* (Stuttgart: Calwer Verlag, 1975), 96.

3. C. S. Mann, *Mark,* in The Anchor Bible, vol. 27 (New York: Doubleday, 1986), 660.

4. William Lane Craig, *Assessing the New Testament Evidence for the Historicity of the Resurrection of Jesus* (Lewiston/Queenston: Mullen, 1989), 198.

5. Norman Perrin, *The Resurrection* (Philadelphia: Fortress, 1977), 31.

6. Roland E. Murphy, O Carm, "Hosea," in *The New Jerome Biblical Commentary* (Englewood Cliffs: Prentice Hall, 1988), 223.

7. There is ambiguity about the number of women mentioned in this text because of the lack of commas in Greek.

8. Craig, *Assessing the New Testament Evidence,* 198.

9. Pierre Benoit, OP, and Marie-Émile Boismard, OP, *Synopse des quatre évangiles en français avec parallèls des apocryphes et des Pères,* Tome II (Paris: Editions du Cerf, 1972).

10. E. P. Sanders, "Synopse des quatre évangiles avec parallèls des apocrypha et des Pères," reviewed in *Journal of Biblical Literature* 94 (1975), 130.

11. Fuller, *Resurrection Narratives,* 52.

12. See Mary R. Thompson, *The Role of Disbelief in Mark* (New York: Paulist, 1989), and J. B. Tyson, "The Blindness of the Disciples in Mark," *Journal of Biblical Literature* 80 (1961), 261–268, among others.

Chapter 4. Mary of Magdala in Luke

1. Robert J. Karris, *Invitation to Luke* (New York: Image, Doubleday, 1977), 102 and 119.

2. David Noel Freedman, ed., *The Anchor Bible Dictionary,* vol. 2 (New York: Doubleday, 1992), 210.

3. Joseph A. Fitzmyer, SJ, *The Gospel according to Luke (I–IX),* The Anchor Bible, vol. 28 (New York: Doubleday, 1981), 695.

4. Harold K. Moulton, *The Analytical Greek Lexicon,* revised edition (Grand Rapids: Zondervan, 1978).

5. Max Zerwick and Mary Grosvenor, *A Grammatical Analysis of the Greek New Testament* (Rome: Biblical Institute Press, 1966), 169.

6. *Anchor Bible Dictionary,* vol. 2, 207.

7. Eberhard Nestle, Erwin Nestle and Kurt Aland, *Novum Testamentum Graece* (New York: American Bible Society, 1993), 242.

8. *Anchor Bible Dictionary,* vol. 2, 207.

9. Ibid., 899.

Chapter 5. Mary of Magdala in the Fourth Gospel

1. See chapter 2, above, 36–43.

2. Raymond E. Brown, SS, *The Community of the Beloved Disciple* (New York: Paulist, 1979), 7.

3. See chapter 2, above, 36–43.

4. Max Zerwick and Mary Grosvenor, *A Grammatical Analysis of the Greek New Testament* (Rome: Biblical Institute Press, 1966), 124.

5. Margaret Davies, *Rhetoric and Reference in the Fourth Gospel* (Sheffield: Sheffield Academic Press, 1992), 335.

6. See, for example, Raymond E. Brown, *The Gospel according to John,* The Anchor Bible, vols. 29, 29a (New York: Doubleday, 1966); Edward Lynn Bode, *The First Easter Morning* (Rome: Biblical Institute Press, 1970); Reginald Fuller, *The Formation of the Resurrection Narratives* (New York: Macmillan, 1971).

7. Frans Neirynck, "John and the Synoptics" in Marinus de Jonge, ed., *L'Evangile de Jean* (Leuven: University Press, 1977), 73–106.

8. Ibid., 104.

9. C. H. Dodd, "The Appearances of the Risen Christ: An Essay in Form Criticism of the Gospels," in *Studies in the Gospels: Essays in Memory of R. H. Lightfoot and D. H. Nineham* (Oxford: Oxford University Press, 1951), 9–35.

10. Brown, *The Gospel according to John,* vol. 2, 984.

11 Nestle-Aland, *Novum Testamentum Graece,* 314–315.

12. Brown, *The Gospel according to John,* vol. 2, 984.

13. John E. Alsup, *The Post-Resurrection Appearance Stories of the Gospel Tradition* (Stuttgart: Calwer Verlag, 1975), 9.

14. Zerwick and Grosvenor, *Grammatical Analysis of the Greek New Testament,* 344.

15. Ibid.

16. See Brown, *The Gospel according to John,* vol. 2, 991–992, and others.

17. Elmer E. Parsons, *Witness to the Resurrection* (Grand Rapids: Baker, 1967), 39.

18. Brown, *The Gospel according to John,* vol. 2, 991–992.

19. Friedrich William Blass and Albert De Brunner, *Greek Grammar of the New Testament* (Chicago: University of Chicago Press, 1962), 169.

20. Ibid., 175.

21. Harold K. Moulton, *The Analytical Greek Lexicon Revised* (Grand Rapids: Zondervan, 1978), 6.

22. Brown, *The Gospel according to John,* vol. 2, 1014.

23. Blass and De Brunner, *Greek Grammar,* 176.

24. Fuller, *Resurrection Narratives,* 101.

25. C. H. Dodd, "The Appearances of the Risen Christ," 20.

26. Ibid., 19.

27. Jerome Neyrey, *The Resurrection Stories* (Wilmington: Glazier, 1988), 75.

Chapter 6. Women Leaders in the Ancient World

1. See Edvard Lohse, *The New Testament Environment* (Nashville: Abingdon, 1974), 207.

2. See Rosemary Ruether, *Religion and Sexism* (New York: Schuster, 1974), 117.

3. Decii Junii Juvenalis, *Fourteen Satires* (Cambridge: Cambridge University Press, 1970), satire 6.

4. See Ludwig Friedlander, *Roman Life and Manners*, vol. 1 (New York: Barnes and Noble, 1907), 237-267.

5. Cornelius Tacitus, *Annals* (New York: Modern Library, 1942), 3:33:34.

6. Friedlander, *Roman Life*, 239.

7. Naphthali Lewis, *Roman Civilization* (New York: Columbia, 1955), 50.

8. Ibid., 52.

9. Arthur E. R. Boak and William G. Sinnig, *A History of Rome to A.D. 565* (New York: Macmillan, 1965), 282.

10. Lewis, *Roman Civilization*, 172.

11. Charles Ryrie, *The Role of Women in the Church* (Chicago: Moody, 1958), 5.

12. Lewis, *Roman Civilization*, 544.

13. Sir James Donaldson, *Woman: Her Position and Influence in Ancient Greece and Rome and among Early Christians* (London: Longmans, 1907), 256.

14. A. H. Smith, "Notes on a Tour in Asia Minor." *Journal of Hellenic Studies* 13 (1887), 256.

15. Pieter W. van der Horst, *Ancient Jewish Epitaphs* (Kampen, Netherlands: Kok Pharos, 1991), 105.

16. Bernadette Brooten, *Women Leaders in the Ancient Synagogues* (Chico: Scholars Press, 1982), 1.

17. Ibid., 137-138.

18. Ibid., 46–51.

19. *The New American Bible* (Nashville: Nelson, 1986), 1157.

20. G. H. R. Horsley, *New Documents Illustrating Early Christianity,* vol. 1 (North Ryde, New South Wales, Australia: Ancient History Documentary Research Centre, 1981), 111–112.

21. Brooten, *Women Leaders,* 158.

22. Horsley, *New Documents,* 1:111.

23. Brooten, *Women Leaders,* 161.

24. Ibid., 86.

25. Brooten, *Women Leaders,* 5, and van der Horst, *Ancient Epitaphs,* 105–106.

26. Brooten, *Women Leaders,* 41.

27. van der Horst, *Ancient Epitaphs,* 105–106.

28. Ibid., 106.

29. Horsley, *New Documents,* 3:33–36.

30. van der Horst, *Ancient Epitaphs,* 92.

31. Brooten, *Women Leaders,* 73.

32. Ibid., 99.

33. Horsley, *New Documents,* 4:239.

34. Ibid.

35. Ibid., 4:240–242.

36. Ibid., 3:34–35.

37. Judith Romney Wegner, *Chattel or Person?* (New York: Oxford, 1988), 5–6.

38. Eugene J. Lipman, *The Mishnah* (New York: Schocken, 1970), 155.

39. Herbert Danby, *The Mishnah* (Oxford: Oxford University Press, 1933), Sotah 3.4:296.

40. Danby, *The Mishnah,* Horayoth 3.7:466.

41. Danby, *The Mishnah,* Aboth 1.5:446.

42. Danby, *The Mishnah,* Tohoroth 7.9:727.

43. Wegner, *Chattel or Person?,* 131.

44. Danby, *The Mishnah,* Ketuboth 7.99:255.

45. Danby, *The Mishnah,* Kiddushim 2.1:323.

46. Wegner, *Chattel or Person?,* 198.

Chapter 7. Women in the Apocryphal and Canonical Literature

1. Walter Bauer, *Orthodoxy and Heresy* (Philadelphia: Fortress, 1971), 193.

2. Wilhelm Schneemelcher, ed., and Edgar Hennecke, *New Testament Apocrypha* (Philadelphia: Westminster, 1959), 189–227.

3. Ibid., 179–187.

4. Ibid., 190.

5. Ibid., 195.

6. Ibid., 195.

7. Ibid., 196.

8. Helmut Koester, *History and Literature of Early Christianity,* vol 2 (Philadelphia: Fortress, 1982), 163.

9. Schneemelcher, *New Testament Apocrypha,* 187.

10. Ibid.

11. James M. Robinson, *The Nag Hammadi Library* (New York: Harper and Row, 1981), 117.

12. Ibid., 120.

13. Ibid., 130.

14. Ibid., 236.

15. Ibid., 235.

16. Elaine Pagels, *The Gnostic Gospels* (New York: Random House, 1979), 66–67.

17. Koester, *History and Literature,* 155.

18. See above, Chapter 5.

19. Robinson, *Nag Hammadi,* 135–136.

20. Schneemelcher, *New Testament Apocrypha,* 247.

21. Robinson, *Nag Hammadi,* 225.

22. Schneemelcher, *New Testament Apocrypha,* 506.

23. James Montague Rhodes, *The Coptic Apocrypha,* 117.

24. Robinson, *Nag Hammadi,* 472.

25. Ibid., 473.

26. Harold K. Moulton, *The Analytical Greek Lexicon Revised* (Grand Rapids: Zondervan, 1977), 388.

27. Robert Banks, *Paul's Idea of Community* (Grand Rapids: Eerdmans, 1980) develops this idea.

28. See Chapter 2 above, 24–28.

Bibliography

Alsup, John E. *The Post-Resurrection Appearance Stories of the Gospel Tradition: A History of Tradition Analysis with Text-Synopsis.* Stuttgart: Calwer Verlag, 1975.

Avi-Yonah, Michael. *The Holy Land.* London: Thames and Hudson, 1972.

Baignet, Michael, Richard Leigh and Henry Lincoln Dell. *Holy Blood, Holy Grail.* Barnes and Noble, 2004.

Banks, Robert. *Paul's Idea of Community.* Grand Rapids: Eerdmans, 1980.

Benoit, Pierre and Marie Émile Boismard. *Synopse des quartre évangiles en français avec parallèls des apocryphes et des Pères,* tome 2. Paris: Editions du Cerf, 1972.

Blass, Frederick William, and Albert De Brunner. *A Greek Grammar of the New Testament.* Chicago: University of Chicago Press, 1961.

Boak, Arthur E. R. and William G. Sinnigen. *A History of Rome to AD 565.* New York: Macmillan, 1965.

Bode, Edward Lynn. *The First Easter Morning.* Rome: Biblical Institute Press, 1970.

Brooke, Rosalind and Christopher, *Popular Religion in the Middle Ages.* London: Thames and Hudson, 1984.

Brooten, Bernadette. *Women Leaders in the Ancient Synagogues.* Chicago: Scholars Press, 1982.

Brown, Dan. *The Da Vinci Code.* New York: Doubleday, 2003.

Brown, Raymond E. *The Community of the Beloved Disciple.* New York: Paulist, 1979.

———. *The Gospel according to John,* The Anchor Bible, vols. 29, 29a. New York: Doubleday, 1966.

———. "Roles of Women in the Fourth Gospel." *Theological Studies* 36 (1975): 688–699.

Bruckberger, Raymond-Leopold. *Mary Magdalene.* New York: Pantheon, 1953.

Buttrick, George A. *Interpreter's Dictionary of the Bible.* Nashville: Abingdon, 1962.

Carnley, Peter. *The Structure of Resurrection Belief.* Oxford: Clarendon, 1987.

Craig, William Lane. *Assessing the New Testament Evidence for the Historicity of the Resurrection of Jesus.* Lewiston/Queenston: Mullen, 1989.

Danby, Herbert. *The Mishnah.* Oxford: Oxford University Press, 1933.

Davies, Margaret. *Rhetoric and Reference in the Fourth Gospel.* Sheffield: Sheffield Academic Press, 1992.

de Voragine, Jacobus. *The Golden Legend.* New York: Longmans, 1941.

Dodd, C. H. "The Appearances of the Risen Christ: An Essay in Form Criticism of the Gospels," in *Studies in the Gospels: Essays in Memory of R. H. Lightfoot and D. H. Nineham.* Oxford: Oxford University Press, 1951.

Donaldson, Sir James. *Woman: Her Position and Influence in Ancient Greece and Rome and among Early Christians.* London: Longmont, 1907.

Douglas, J. D., ed. *New Bible Dictionary,* 2nd ed. Wheaton: Tyndale, 1982.

Ephraim the Syrian, "Homily on Our Lord," in *Nicene and Post-Nicene Fathers of the Christian Church,* edited by Philip Schaff and Henry Wace, vol. 13. Grand Rapids: Eerdmans, 1983.

Fitzmyer, Joseph. *The Gospel according to Luke I–IX,* The Anchor Bible, vol. 28. New York: Doubleday, 1981.

Freedman, David Noel, ed. *The Anchor Bible Dictionary,* 6 vols. New York: Doubleday, 1992.

Friedlander, Ludwig. *Roman Life and Manners,* vol. 1. New York: Barnes and Noble, 1907.

Fuller, Reginald H. *The Formation of the Resurrection Narratives.* New York: Macmillan, 1971.

Gauer, Rivka. *Biblical Holy Places: An Illustrated Guide.* London: A. E. Black, Ltd. 1987.

Geldenhuys, Norval. *Commentary on the Gospel of Luke.* Grand Rapids: Eerdmans, 1956.

Grassi, Carolyn and Joseph. *Mary Magdalene and the Women in Jesus' Life.* Kansas City: Sheed and Ward, 1986.

Gryson, Roger. *The Ministry of Women in the Early Church.* Collegeville: Liturgical Press, 1976.

Harrington, Daniel, SJ. "The Gospel according to Mark." In *New Jerome Biblical Commentary,* edited by Raymond E. Brown, Joseph A. Fitzmyer, and Roland E. Murphy, 596–629. Englewood Cliffs: Prentice-Hall, 1990.

Horsely, G. H. R. *New Documents Illustrating Early Christianity,* 4 vols. North Ryde, New South Wales, Australia: Ancient History Documentary Research Centre, 1981.

James, Montague Rhodes. *The Apocryphal New Testament.* Oxford: Oxford University Press, 1924.

Juvenalis, Decii Junii . "Satire 6," in *Fourteen Satires.* Cambridge: University of Cambridge Press, 1970.

Karris, Robert J. *Invitation to Luke.* New York: Image-Doubleday, 1977.

Koester, Helmut. *History and Literature of Early Christianity.* Philadelphia: Fortress, 1982.

Lawson, R. P. *Origen: the Song of Songs.* New York: Newman, 1957.

Lewis, Naphthali. *Roman Civilization.* New York: Columbia, 1955.

Lipman, Eugene J. *The Mishnah.* New York: Schocken, 1970.

Lohse, Eduard. *The New Testament Environment.* Nashville: Abingdon, 1974.

Maier, Paul L. *Josephus: The Essential Writings.* Grand Rapids: Kregal Publications, 1988.

Malvern, Marjorie. *Venus in Sackcloth.* Carbondale: Southern Illinois University Press, 1975.

Mann, C. S. *Mark,* The Anchor Bible, vol. 27. New York: Doubleday, 1986.

Mierow, Charles C., trans. *The Letters of St. Jerome.* New York: Newman, 1963.

Metzger, Bruce M. *A Textual Commentary on the Greek New Testament.* London: United Bible Societies, 1971.

Moulton, Harold K. *The Analytical Greek Lexicon,* revised. Grand Rapids: Zondervan, 1977.

Murphy, Roland E., O Carm, "Hosea." In *The New Jerome Biblical Commentary,* 217–228. Englewood Cliffs: Prentice-Hall, 1990.

Mycoff, David. *The Life of Saint Mary Magdalene and of Her Sister Saint Martha.* Kalamazoo: Cistercian Publications, 1989.

Neirynck, Frans. "John and the Synoptics." In *L'evangile de Jean,* edited by Marinus de Jonge. Leuven: Leuven University Press, 1977.

Neyrey, Jerome. *The Resurrection Stories.* Wilmington: Glazier, 1988.

Pagels, Elaine. *The Gnostic Gospels.* New York: Random House, 1979.

Parsons, Elmer E. *Witness to the Resurrection.* Grand Rapids: Baker, 1967.

Perrin, Norman. *The Resurrection.* Philadelphia: Fortress, 1977.

Ridderbos, Herman. *Paul: An Outline of His Theology.* Grand Rapids: Eerdmans, 1975.

Robinson, James M. *The Nag Hammadi Library.* New York: Harper and Row, 1981.

Ruether, Rosemary. *Religion and Sexism.* New York: Schuster, 1974.

Ryrie, Charles. *The Role of Women in the Church.* Chicago: Moody, 1958.

Sanders, E. P. *Jesus and Judaism.* London: SCM, 1985.

———. "Synopse des quatre évangiles avec parallèls des apocryphe et des Pères," review in *Journal of Biblical Literature* 94 (1975):130.

Saxer, Viktor. *Le Culte de Marie Madeleine en Occident, dès Origines à la Fin du Moyen-Age,* 2 vols. Paris: Librarie Clavreuil, 1959.

Schaberg, Jane. "How Mary Magdalene Became a Whore." *Bible Review* 8:5 (1992), 30–37.

Schneemelcher, Wilhelm, ed., and Edgar Hennecke. *New Testament Apocrypha,* vol. 1. Philadelphia: Westminster, 1963.

Smith, A. H. "Notes on a Tour in Asia Minor." *Journal of Hellenic Studies* 13 (1887): 256.

Straw, Carole. *Gregory the Great.* Berkeley: University of California Press, 1988.

Sumption, Jonathon. *Pilgrimage: An Image of Medieval Religion.* Totowa, NJ: Rowman and Littlefield, 1975.

Tacitus, Cornelius. *Annals.* New York: Modern Library, 1942.

Tetlow, Elizabeth M. *Women and Ministry in the New Testament.* New York: Paulist, 1980.

Thompson, Mary R. *The Role of Disbelief in Mark.* New York: Paulist, 1989.

Tyson, J. B. "The Blindness of the Disciples in Mark." *Journal of Biblical Literature* 80 (1981): 261–268.

van der Horst, Pieter W. *Ancient Jewish Epitaphs.* Kohl Pharos: Kampen, 1991.

Warner, Marina. *Alone of All Her Sex.* New York: Vintage, 1976.

Wegner, Judith Romney. *Chattel or Person?* New York: Oxford, 1988.

Wilcken, Ulrich. "The Tradition History of the Resurrection of Jesus." In *The Significance of the Message of the Resurrection for Faith in Jesus Christ,* edited by C. F. D. Moule. London: SCM, 1968.

Zerwick, Max and Mary Grosvenor. *A Grammatical Analysis of the Greek New Testament.* Rome: Biblical Institute Press, 1966.

Index